W9-CLD-415

The 20th Century's
Most Influential
HISPANICS

Frida Kahlo
Mexican Portrait Artist

Titles in the series include:

Carlos Santana, Legendary Guitarist
Che Guevara, Revolutionary
Dolores Huerta, Labor Leader
Rigoberta Menchu, Indian Rights Activist
Robert Clemente, Baseball Hall of Famer
Ellen Ochoa, First Female Hispanic Astronaut
Diego Rivera, Muralist

Frida Kahlo
Mexican Portrait Artist

by Laurie Collier Hillstrom

LUCENT BOOKS

A part of Gale, Cengage Learning

GALE
CENGAGE Learning

Detroit • New York • San Francisco • New Haven, Conn • Waterville, Maine • London

GALE
CENGAGE Learning™

LIBRARY OF CONGRESS CATALOGING-IN-PUBLICATION DATA

Hillstrom, Laurie Collier, 1965-
 Frida Kahlo : painter / by Laurie Collier Hillstrom.
   p. cm. -- (The twentieth century's most influential Hispanics)
 Includes bibliographical references and index.
 ISBN-13: 978-1-4205-0019-6 (hardcover)
 1. Kahlo, Frida--Juvenile literature. 2. Painters--Mexico--Biography--Juvenile literature. I. Title.
  ND259.K33H55 2007
  759.972--dc2
                                                          [B]
                                                  2007032106

Lucent Books
27500 Drake Rd
Farmington Hills MI 48331

ISBN-13: 978-1-4205-0019-6
ISBN-10: 1-4205-0019-8

Printed in the United States of America
2 3 4 5 6 7 12 11 10 09 08

Table of Contents

Foreword

Hispanics in America and elsewhere have shed humble beginnings to soar to impressive and previously unreachable heights. In the twenty-first century, influential Hispanic figures can be found worldwide and in all fields of endeavor including science, politics, education, the arts, sports, religion, and literature. Some accomplishments, like those of musician Carlos Santana or author Alisa Valdes-Rodriguez, have added a much-needed Hispanic voice to the artistic landscape. Others, such as revolutionary Che Guevara or labor leader Dolores Huerta, have spawned international social movements that have enriched the rights of all peoples.

But who exactly is Hispanic? When studying influential Hispanics, it is important to understand what the term actually means. Unlike strictly racial categories like "black" or "Asian," the term "Hispanic" joins a huge swath of people from different countries, religions, and races. The category was first used by the U.S. census bureau in 1980 and is used to refer to Spanish-speaking people of any race. Officially, it denotes a person whose ancestry either descends in whole or in part from the people of Spain or from the various peoples of Spanish-speaking Latin America. Often the term "Hispanic" is used synonymously with the term "Latino," but the two actually have slightly different meanings. "Latino" refers only to people from the countries of Latin America, such as Argentina, Brazil, and Venezuela, whether they speak Spanish or Portuguese. Meanwhile, Hispanic refers only to Spanish-speaking peoples but from any Spanish-speaking country, such as Spain, Puerto Rico, or Mexico.

In America, Hispanics are reaching new heights of cultural influence, buying power, and political clout. More than 35 million people identified themselves as Hispanic on the 2000 U.S. census, and there were estimated to be more than 41 million Hispanics in America as of 2006. In the twenty-first century people of Hispanic origin have officially become the nation's largest ethnic minority, outnumbering both blacks and Asians. Hispanics constitute about 13 percent of the nation's total population, and by 2050 their numbers are expected to rise to 102.6 million, at which point they would account for 24 percent of the total population. With growing numbers and expanding influence, Hispanic leaders, artists, politicians, and scientists in America and in other countries are commanding attention like never before.

These unique and fascinating stories are the subjects of *The Twentieth Century's Most Influential Hispanics* collection from Lucent Books. Each volume in the series critically examines the challenges, accomplishments, and legacy of influential Hispanic figures; many of whom, like Alberto Gonzales, sprang from modest beginnings to achieve groundbreaking goals. *The Twentieth Century's Most Influential Hispanics* offers vivid narrative, fully documented primary and secondary source quotes, a bibliography, thorough index, and mix of color and black-and-white photographs which enhance each volume and provide excellent starting points for research and discussion.

Introduction

Expressing Feelings through Art

The Mexican artist Frida Kahlo created fewer than two hundred paintings in her lifetime, and more than half of these works are self-portraits. Kahlo's intense, highly personal, and often disturbing paintings frequently explore the constant physical pain she endured as a result of an accident. Many paintings also delve into the deep emotional pain she experienced during her marriage to the famous mural painter Diego Rivera. "I paint my own reality," she once said. "The only thing I know is that I paint because I need to, and I paint whatever passes through my head without any other consideration."[1]

Art historians agree that Kahlo's work cannot be understood fully without examining the turbulent years she spent with Rivera, who remains the best-known Mexican painter of the twentieth century. Rivera loved Kahlo and helped her gain entrance into a glamorous world of global travel and exciting art. But Rivera also mistreated his wife in numerous ways. He often took Kahlo for granted, routinely placed greater importance on his artistic career than on his relationship with her, and cheated on her with other women throughout their many years together. These blows took a heavy toll on Kahlo, who was a proud and ambitious artist in her own

Many art critics now agree that Frida Kahlo has become one of the icons of twentieth-century art.

right. In the end, though, their complex relationship—and Kahlo's refusal to surrender to the feelings of sadness and bitterness that shadowed her during her time with Rivera—inspired her to create some of her most powerful and enduring works of art.

In addition to expressing her innermost feelings about love and betrayal, Kahlo's art also reflects her pride in her Mexican heritage. Kahlo grew up during the decade-long Mexican Revolution, when the nation's poor and indigenous people fought to close racial and economic divisions in Mexican society and gain more influence in government. Kahlo incorporated many elements of Mexican history and culture in her work. She also demonstrated her passion for the country and its people in the colorful, traditional clothing she often wore.

Kahlo's life and work hold tremendous interest for art lovers and critics, partly because both the person and her paintings are filled with contradictions. Kahlo rarely appeared in public without her colorful outfits and elaborate jewelry, for instance, but her festive appearance concealed a lifetime of severe physical and emotional pain. Similarly, Kahlo often depicted herself in self-portraits as strong and determined, but her art also reflected the great turmoil

Frida Kahlo and Diego Rivera's turbulent marriage had a tremendous impact on Kahlo's artwork.

and suffering that she experienced. One art historian noted:

> The palpable energy that radiates from Kahlo's small, meticulously observed self-portraits comes from the ferocity of her dialogue with herself and the directness with which she told her story. She painted herself cracked open, weeping beside her extracted heart, hemorrhaging during a miscarriage, anesthetized on a hospital [bed, and] sleeping with a skeleton.[2]

Although Kahlo struggled to gain recognition as an artist during her lifetime, her work has grown increasingly popular since her death in 1954. In fact, she has attracted a devoted worldwide following and become one of the icons of twentieth-century art. As one critic explained the remarkable appeal of Kahlo's work, "she created haunting, sensual, and stunningly original paintings that fused elements of surrealism, fantasy, and folklore into powerful narratives."[3]

Chapter 1

Child of the Revolution

In creating her famous self-portraits and other paintings, Frida Kahlo frequently drew upon her childhood and family background. As a mestiza, or Mexican of mixed European and Indian ancestry, she often explored the different parts of her ethnic heritage in her art. She also used her painting as a way to express complicated feelings about her relationship with her parents and to recall the pain and loneliness she experienced during a serious childhood illness.

To a large extent, Kahlo's life and work were also shaped by events in Mexican history that took place during her youth. She was born just three years before the start of the Mexican Revolution, a decade-long conflict in which poor and working-class Mexicans tried to gain greater influence in the nation's government. Kahlo became a strong supporter of the revolution's principles, and she celebrated many aspects of her Mexican identity and culture in her art.

A Mixed Ethnic Heritage

Kahlo was born on July 6, 1907, in Coyoacán, a quiet, leafy

13

suburb of Mexico City, the capital of Mexico. Her full name at birth was Magdalena Carmen Frieda Kahlo y Calderón, but her family and friends always called her Frida. She changed the spelling of her name from the German "Frieda" to the Spanish "Frida" during the 1930s.

Like most people in Mexico, Kahlo came from an ethnic background known as mestiza. Her father, Guillermo Kahlo, had been born in Germany to Hungarian Jewish parents. He had immigrated to Mexico in 1891, at the age of 19. Her mother, Matilde Calderón y González, was half Indian and half Spanish. Kahlo's parents met in the late 1890s, when they worked together at a jewelry store, and married in 1898.

Kahlo was the third of four girls in her family. She had two older sisters, Matilde (known as Matita) and Adriana, and one younger sister, Cristina (known as Cristi). Kahlo was only a few months old when her mother became pregnant with Cristina. Perhaps due to the physical demands of the new pregnancy, her mother chose not to breastfeed Kahlo herself and instead hired an Indian woman to serve as a wet nurse. Some people who have studied Kahlo's life and career claim that this experience proved emotionally damaging for her. They suggest that being breastfed by someone other than her own mother created feelings of rejection and abandonment that affected Kahlo for the rest of her life.

Throughout her youth, Kahlo also struggled under her mother's strict rules and religious discipline. A devout Catholic, Matilde Kahlo expected her daughters to attend church regularly and to offer thanks to God before every meal. Kahlo did not share her mother's faith and often rebelled against it. "My mother was hysterical about religion," she recalled. "We had to pray before meals. While others concentrated on their inner selves, Cristi and I would look at each other, forcing ourselves not to laugh."[4]

Kahlo's mother also insisted that her daughters learn how to sew, cook, and clean. Matilde Kahlo believed that all young women should develop domestic skills so they would be prepared to deal with any tough times they experienced. But Kahlo, as an independent-minded tomboy, did not find such things to be important. She felt that young women should pursue education in order to break out of traditional gender roles. She chafed under her mother's rules and secretly referred to Matilde as "mi jefe" (my chief).

Hernán Cortés arrived in Mexico in 1519, thus beginning Spain's rule of the country for the next three centuries.

In contrast to her difficult relationship with her mother, Kahlo felt a deep love and respect for her father. Guillermo Kahlo was a highly intelligent man who enjoyed playing classical piano and reading the works of great philosophers and poets. Kahlo admired his clear-minded, questioning approach toward politics and religion. Although Guillermo suffered from epilepsy—a condition in which damage to the brain or nervous system occasionally causes victims to fall unconscious and have convulsions or seizures—he still managed to build a successful career as a photographer. He eventually saved enough money to build a house for his growing family in Coyoacán. Since the outside of the dwelling was painted a bright, cobalt blue, it became known as the Blue House.

Kahlo enjoyed growing up in this house, largely because of the close relationship she developed with her father. She wrote in her diary:

> My childhood was marvelous because, although my father was a sick man (he had vertigos [fainting spells or seizures] every month and a half), he was an immense example to me of tenderness, of work (photographer and also painter), and above all of understanding for all my problems.[5]

The Mexican Revolution

Shortly before Kahlo's birth, her father had been hired by the Mexican government to photograph some of the nation's most important architectural sites. He spent several years traveling around the country and visiting historic landmarks, including the remnants of ancient Toltec, Mayan, and Aztec civilizations. These native peoples had ruled Mexico for thousands of years before Spanish explorers, led by the ruthless Hernán Cortés, arrived in 1519. The period before the Spaniards arrived is known as the pre-Hispanic or pre-Conquest period in Mexican history.

Using guns and horses—neither of which the native people had ever seen before—Cortés and his men conquered large parts of Mexico. In 1521, the Spaniards captured Tenochtitlán, the capital of the Aztec empire, and took control of the country. Spain ruled Mexico for the next three centuries, which is known as the Colonial period in Mexican history. During this time, the Spanish rulers converted many Indians to Catholicism and also imposed many changes to Mexican culture. In addition, most of the country's farmland was taken away from Indians and peasants and placed into huge estates, or haciendas, controlled by wealthy Spaniards.

The movement for Mexican independence from Spain started in 1810, when a Catholic priest, Father Miguel Hidalgo, led thousands of Indians in protest marches. Although the Spanish rulers executed Hidalgo in 1811, a string of other revolutionary leaders emerged to take up the cause over the next ten years. Mexico finally gained its independence from Spain in 1821, but the young nation struggled to pay debts owed to the United States and several European nations. Some of these countries took advantage of Mexico as a source of cheap labor and natural resources. In the mid-1800s, Mexico ended up as a colony of France for nearly a decade.

When France withdrew its troops from Mexico in 1867 after years of bloodshed, a revolutionary leader named Benito Juárez became president of Mexico. His rule lasted only until 1872, however, when he died of a heart attack. Four years of political instability followed until November 21, 1876, when General Porfirio Díaz and his rebel army marched into Mexico City to claim power. This marked the beginning of Díaz's thirty-four-year reign over Mexico.

After seizing power, Díaz used threats and violence to silence his critics and political opponents. One of the weapons he used

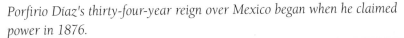

Porfirio Díaz's thirty-four-year reign over Mexico began when he claimed power in 1876.

to frighten and control the people of Mexico was the rurales, a police force that patrolled the countryside in order to stamp out any signs of rebellion among poor peasants and Indians. The Díaz government broke up labor unions in order to limit the power of workers and keep wages low. It also gave land and money to the president's wealthy political allies and left the nation's poor to fend for themselves.

Simmering anger toward the Díaz government finally boiled over in 1910. After arresting his most visible political opponent, Francisco Indalecio Madero, Díaz announced that he had been elected to serve yet another term in office as president of Mexico. The questionable election results turned out to be the last straw for many long-suffering Mexicans. Fighting broke out across the country between government troops and rebel forces under three regional leaders—Pascual Orozco, Pancho Villa, and Emiliano Zapata—marking the start of the decade-long Mexican Revolution.

Shaped by the Revolution

Although Kahlo was only three years old when the revolution began, this important turning point in her nation's history made a major impact on her life. When Díaz fell from power in 1911, for instance, her father lost his job photographing historic sites for the Mexican government. It was hard for Guillermo Kahlo to find work during the turbulent war years, and the family struggled to make ends meet. They were forced to rent out rooms in the Blue House and sell many of their possessions in order to pay their bills.

As a young girl, Kahlo often heard gunshots in her neighborhood and saw soldiers running through the streets. On a few occasions, rebel fighters came into the courtyard garden of the Blue House to hide, and Matilde Kahlo fed them warm tortillas. As Kahlo got older, she developed a deep sympathy for the revolutionaries who wanted to give poor and working-class people greater influence in government. In fact, she identified so strongly with the principles of the Mexican Revolution that she often claimed to have been born in 1910—the opening year of the conflict—instead of 1907. "Frida Kahlo apparently decided that she and the new Mexico were born at the same time,"[6] explained one art historian.

A True Mexican

[Frida Kahlo] was a woman who related extremely vividly to her environment. She had a complex but deeply satisfying rapport with her fellow Mexicans of all classes and races.... She relished the country of her birth, and its tragic history, with an enthusiasm that sometimes bordered on the fetishistic [obsessive].

Robin Richmond, *Painters and Places: Frida Kahlo in Mexico*. San Francisco: Pomegranate Artbooks, 1994, p. 12.

Marked by Childhood Illness

Another defining event of Kahlo's childhood occurred during the war years, when she contracted polio at the age of six. Poliomyelitis is a virus that infects the brain and spinal cord, causing a high fever and sometimes paralysis (loss of movement). Polio was common, especially among children, until scientists developed a preventative vaccine during the second half of the twentieth century. The disease left many young victims deformed or disabled due to nerve and muscle damage.

Until she caught polio, Kahlo was a very social and active child. But the disease, and her long and difficult recovery from it, forced her to remain in her bedroom for nine months. During this time, Kahlo invented an imaginary friend to help her deal with feelings of loneliness and isolation, as she recalled in her diary:

> I must have been 6 years old when I experienced intensely an imaginary friendship with a little girl more or less the same age as me. I do not remember her image or her color. But I do know that she was gay—she laughed a lot. Without sounds. She was agile and she danced as if she weighed nothing at all. I followed her in all her movements and while she danced I told her my secret problems.[7]

By the time Kahlo was allowed to leave her room, the effects of polio had made her right leg thinner and shorter than her left. She tried to disguise these problems by wearing a special shoe with a lift in the heel and hiding her leg under long pants or skirts. Other kids still noticed and teased her about it, though, calling her "Peg-leg Frida."

Kahlo's father encouraged her to build up the muscles in her leg through exercise. At a time when few girls played sports, he encouraged her to try football, wrestling, soccer, boxing, and swimming. Kahlo and her father also went for long nature walks together. They collected interesting leaves and insects and took them home to examine and sketch. Guillermo Kahlo also taught his young daughter how to use a camera, develop film, and retouch photographs. She applied some of these skills to her later work as an artist.

Supporting Mexicanidad

Despite missing a year of school due to illness, Kahlo was an excellent student. She attended Colegio Alemán, a German primary school in Coyoacán, where she enjoyed studying art, science, and literature. Thanks to her great memory, she also learned to read and speak Spanish, German, and English during her early school years.

In 1920, when Kahlo was thirteen years old, the Mexican Revolution finally came to an end. General Álvaro Obregón became president of Mexico and immediately began making reforms under a new constitution. His government distributed land to poor people, increased wages and rights for workers, and made significant improvements in the areas of health care and education.

Of all the changes made by Obregón, the one that had the biggest impact on Kahlo and other students was his appointment of reformer José Vasconcelos as Minister of Education. Vasconcelos believed that every Mexican—rich or poor, Indian or European, male or female—deserved access to a free, high-quality education. His first step toward achieving this goal involved opening the country's top schools to all qualified students. Vasconcelos also wanted to make art, literature, and other elements of culture more accessible to the ordinary people of Mexico. Toward this end, he launched a government-sponsored program to put the work of Mexican artists on display in public places.

The fundamental idea behind Vasconcelos's programs was Mexicanidad, or the celebration of Mexican history, culture, and

The reforms made under General Álavaro Obregón allowed Kahlo to attend Mexico's National Preparatory School.

identity. The Mexicanidad movement rejected European influences and placed a new emphasis on authentic Mexican traditions, such as pre-Hispanic art and Indian crafts. Kahlo became a wholehearted supporter of Mexicanidad, both as a student and later as an artist. "Outspoken in her commitment to the ideals of that long and bloody struggle [the Mexican Revolution], Kahlo expressed her ties to what she called la raza, or the people, not only in her art but in her dress [and] her behavior,"[8] noted one biographer.

Promoter of Education, the Arts, and Mexicanidad

José Vasconcelos was a reform-minded Mexican official who served as minister of education under President Álvaro Obregón in the 1920s. He was instrumental in increasing government support for education and the arts, and in launching the cultural movement known as Mexicanidad.

Vasconcelos was born on February 28, 1882, in Oaxaca, Mexico. During the Mexican Revolution, he fought under revolutionary leader Francisco Madero, who helped remove dictator Porfirio Díaz from power in 1911. Madero then took control of the government, but his reign lasted only two years. When Madero fell from power, Vasconcelos went into exile.

Vaconcelos returned to Mexico at the end of the Revolution in 1920, when Álvaro Obregón was elected president. He became the director of the National University of Mexico and also served as Obregón's minister of education. In this position, Vasconcelos launched an ambitious program to increase literacy rates and give all Mexicans access to a free, high-quality education. As one step in this program, Vasconcelos opened the country's top schools to all qualified students, which allowed Kahlo to enroll at the previously all-male National Preparatory School.

Vasconcelos also developed a government-sponsored mural-painting program to put the work of Mexican artists on display in public places. Kahlo's future husband, Diego Rivera, took advantage of this opportunity to use murals to teach the Mexican people about their history. All of these efforts were part of Mexicanidad, which encouraged the Mexican people to reject European influences and celebrate their own unique identity and culture.

Political pressures forced Vasconcelos to resign from his post as minister of education in 1924. He went back into exile until 1929, when he made a failed bid for the presidency of Mexico. Vasconcelos died in Mexico City on June 30, 1959.

José Vasconcelos was Álvaro Obregón's minister of education and played a major role in Kahlo's and Rivera's meeting.

A Rebellious Student

After completing her primary-school education, Kahlo entered the Escuela Nacional Preparatoria (National Preparatory School) in Mexico City in 1922, at the age of 15. Her enrollment at this secondary school—widely considered to be the best in the country—was possible because Vasconcelos had recently opened its doors to female students for the first time. After passing the tough entrance exam, Kahlo was proud to become one of only thirty-five girls among two thousand students in her class. She planned to study biology, anatomy, and other life sciences in order to become a doctor or an illustrator of medical textbooks.

Kahlo loved her time as a student at the National Preparatory School. After years of rebelling against her mother's rules, she rel-

Kahlo first met Diego Rivera when she was a student at the National Preparatory School and he was painting a large mural there.

ished the freedom of traveling alone by trolley an hour each day to the middle of Mexico City. She enjoyed browsing in the busy shops, being entertained by street musicians, and spending time with fellow students from different backgrounds. She found it very exciting to discuss important issues—like politics, race, and national identity—with other young people in the years following the end of the revolution.

Many students at the National Preparatory School formed clubs or cliques based on their different interests. Kahlo joined a group called the Cachuchas (peaked caps), which was known for playing pranks on teachers and generally showing a lack of respect for authority and rules. She soon became involved in a romantic relationship with the leader of the group, a bright, handsome, well-spoken young man named Alejandro Gómez Arias.

Kahlo and the Cachuchas particularly enjoyed playing tricks on Diego Rivera, a well-known artist who had been hired to paint a large mural at the National Preparatory School as part of Vasconcelos's Mexicanidad program. Born in 1886 in Guanajuato, Mexico, Rivera had shown great promise as an artist from an early age. In 1906, he traveled to Europe, where he spent the next fifteen years studying great works of art, socializing with famous artists, and experimenting with different painting styles. By the time he returned to Mexico in 1921, following the end of the revolution, Rivera had settled upon wall-sized murals as the style best suited to expressing his liberal views on Mexican politics, history, and culture.

Kahlo often teased the big, friendly artist as he stood on a high scaffold and tried to concentrate on his work. She also stole his lunch and soaped the steps of his ladder. Like many other women, however, Kahlo found herself strangely drawn to Rivera, despite his homely appearance. In fact, she informed her friends that she planned to have his baby someday. Unfortunately for Kahlo, this plan, along with her education and all of her future goals, were soon thrown into doubt when she was involved in a serious accident.

Chapter 2

A Life-Changing Accident

In 1925, at the age of eighteen, Frida Kahlo was seriously injured when the bus she was riding on her way home from school was hit by a trolley. This terrible accident changed the course of her life. The injuries forced Kahlo to stay in bed for more than a year, often with her body encased in a plaster cast. Her paintings expressed her feelings of pain, fear, and loneliness.

Looking Forward

During the summer of 1925, Kahlo looked forward to completing her final year of study at the National Preparatory School and then going to college. The eighteen-year-old enjoyed the stimulating intellectual atmosphere of her school in the years following the end of the Mexican Revolution. She also loved her carefree life as a student and the freedom it offered from the watchful eye of her mother.

Since her father had struggled to find work during the war years, Kahlo's family did not have much money to pay for her education. In order to help out, Kahlo worked at a series of summer jobs in a pharmacy, a factory, and a lumberyard. She did not last long in any of these jobs, however, because she found them so boring. Her father eventually found her a position as an apprentice to a printer, Fernando Fernandez. Kahlo enjoyed the work, which involved copying prints of works by famous painters, and began to develop her own talents as an artist.

During this time, Kahlo also took advantage of her newfound freedom to explore her strong, rebellious side. She liked to behave in ways that shocked people. For instance, she often dressed up in men's clothing and pretended to be a boy. It also was at this time that Kahlo began to indulge in intimate relationships with several men.

Dancing with Death

Kahlo's carefree existence and bright future suddenly changed on the afternoon of September 17, 1925. The life-changing series of events started when she and Arias ran through the rain-slick streets of Mexico City to catch a bus home from school. Although motorized buses were a relatively new addition to the city's traffic, they had quickly drawn passengers away from the older, slower electric trolley system. Unfortunately for Kahlo, many of the bus drivers were young and inexperienced and took foolish chances, including the one who was driving the bus she boarded that day.

Shortly after Kahlo and Arias got on the bus, it approached a major intersection. The passengers noticed a trolley coming toward the intersection from another direction. The bus driver hurried to cross in front of the trolley, but his hasty decision had disastrous consequences. The heavy trolley crashed into the side of the bus with tremendous force, then pushed the bus sideways until it hit the wall of a building and broke into pieces. Many passengers were thrown from the bus or trapped in the wreckage. Several people died at the scene, and many others suffered severe injuries.

In the confusion following the accident, Arias woke up underneath the trolley. He managed to climb out and started to look for Kahlo. He found her lying on the ground, her body naked and bleeding and covered with a fine gold dust. "Frida was totally nude," he recalled. "The collision had unfastened her clothes.

Someone in the bus … had been carrying a packet of powdered gold…. The gold fell all over the bleeding body of Frida."[9] A child who saw the accident scene said the sparkly powder made Frida look like a ballerina.

Although Kahlo was conscious, she was clearly in shock and had a metal handrail sticking out of her abdomen. "The handrail went through me like a sword through a bull,"[10] she explained later. When a workman who happened to be passing by pulled the piece of metal out of her belly, she screamed so loudly that witnesses claimed she drowned out the sirens of approaching emergency vehicles.

Arias carried Kahlo across the street to a pool hall and attended to her until an ambulance arrived. She was taken to a nearby Red Cross Hospital and rushed into emergency surgery. Her injuries were so numerous and severe that doctors held out little hope for her survival. Kahlo's spine was broken in three places, her right leg was fractured in eleven places, and her right foot was dislocated and crushed. She also broke her collarbone, several ribs, and her pelvis. The metal handrail pierced her kidney and reproductive organs and caused severe bleeding.

Facing a Long, Painful Recovery

When Kahlo woke up hours later, she found herself in a crowded, dingy hospital ward for patients who did not have the money to pay for a private room. Most of her body was enclosed in a box-like plaster cast that resembled a coffin. This situation seemed strangely appropriate to Kahlo, who came to believe that she might well die from her injuries. "In this hospital, death dances around my bed at night,"[11] she wrote in a letter to Arias.

For the first few weeks, the only member of her family who could bear to see Kahlo in this condition was her oldest sister. "Matilde saw the account [of the accident] in the newspapers and was the first to come, and she didn't leave me for three months; day and night she was at my side," Kahlo remembered. "My mother was speechless for a month because of the effect and did not come to see me. When my sister Adriana heard about it, she fainted. It caused my father so much sadness that he took sick and could only come to see me three weeks later."[12]

Kahlo's fondness for painting self-portraits, like this one titled Self-Portrait with a Monkey (1940), *began as she was recovering from her serious accident.*

Kahlo hoped that Arias would stay by her side as she recovered, but he showed little interest in continuing their relationship following the accident. Nevertheless, Kahlo poured out her emotions in long, detailed letters to him.

You can't imagine how desperate a person gets with this sickness; I feel a frightful discomfort that I can't explain, and there's also a pain that nothing can stop. I can't write much because I can hardly bend, I can't walk because my leg hurts horribly, I'm tired of reading—I don't have anything good to read—and all I can do is cry, and sometimes I can't even do that.[13]

Painting as Therapy

After spending a month in the hospital, Kahlo was finally allowed to go home. She still faced a long and difficult recovery, however, and was confined to her bed in a plaster body cast for several more months. Kahlo took up painting during this time as a way to relieve her boredom and concentrate on something other than her pain.

> For many years my father had kept a box of oil paints and some paintbrushes in an old jar and a palette in the corner of his photographic studio. Ever since I was a little girl, as the saying goes, I'd had my eye on that box of paints. I couldn't explain why. Being confined to bed for so long, I finally took the opportunity to ask my father for it.[14]

With her torso in a stiff cast, Kahlo could not sit or stand upright to paint. Her mother solved this problem by building a special easel that attached to the side of the bed, allowing Kahlo to paint while lying down. Being stuck in bed also limited the subjects available for Kahlo to paint, so her mother placed a mirror above her head and encouraged her to paint self-portraits.

Kahlo spent many hours looking at herself in the mirror and painting portraits that not only captured her physical appearance, but also explored her emotional state. "During her time confined to bed, Frida Kahlo had the opportunity to make an intensive study of her own mirror image," noted one biographer. "This self-analysis took place at a time when, having only recently escaped death, she was starting to discover and experience both her own self and the world about her at a new and more conscious level."[15] In this way, painting offered Kahlo a way to create a new identity for herself.

Since Kahlo started painting at a time when she was enduring severe pain, her artistic works often expressed her suffering or her determination to overcome it. "The dramatization of her suffering through painting became her self-image, a cry of pain and a demand for attention, which in real life she spared her friends,"[16] one art critic explained.

Paints the Unfulfilled

As the accident changed my path, many things prevented me from fulfilling the desires which everyone considers normal, and to me nothing seemed more normal than to paint what had not been fulfilled.

Frida Kahlo, quoted in Jill A. Laidlaw, *Artists in Their Time: Frida Kahlo.* New York: Franklin Watts, 2003, p. 42

Suffers a Relapse

Kahlo's condition gradually improved until she was finally able to leave her bedroom in early 1926. After months of immobility, she was pleased to be able to get around by herself again. Unfortunately for Kahlo, however, the doctors had not discovered the full extent of her injuries. During the summer of 1926, she began suffering from severe back pains. X-rays revealed that three vertebrae in her spine remained out of place. Once again, Kahlo was placed in a plaster cast and forced to return to bed for several months.

During this second span of time in bed, Kahlo completed what is considered to be her first mature work, *Self-Portrait in a Velvet Dress*. Influenced by the formal style of portrait painting long used by European artists, it shows Kahlo in a traditional pose and wearing elegant clothing. It also incorporates several elements that became trademarks of her later work, including eyebrows that meet above her nose, and a steady gaze directed at the viewer. Kahlo intended the painting to be a gift for her estranged boyfriend, Arias. "Like all the self-portraits that followed, the painting was a gift meant to join the artist and a loved one, a kind of talisman against Frida's constant fear that people wouldn't remember her, that she was unloved."[17]

Kahlo painted Self-Portrait in a Velvet Dress *during her second time being confined to bed after her trolley accident.*

Although she frequently explored the effects of the accident on her physical and emotional health, Kahlo found it too painful to address the life-changing event directly in her work. In fact, she only portrayed the accident in her art once, exactly a year after it occurred. In September 1926, Kahlo drew a rough pencil sketch titled *Accident* that pictured the bus, the trolley, and her own broken body lying on the ground.

Participating in Politics

By early 1927, Kahlo had once again recovered enough to get out of bed and move around by herself. She still endured pain in her leg, however, and had to wear a brace to support her back. These continuing problems convinced her that she did not have the strength and energy she needed to return to school. She gave up her dream of studying medicine and began thinking about trying to build a career as an artist.

Without the demands of attending school full time, Kahlo was able to pay more attention to political developments that were taking place in Mexico and around the world. As her health improved, Kahlo began attending weekly gatherings of artists, writers, and intellectuals at the home of Tina Modotti. Modotti was an American photographer who was best known for taking pictures of poor and working people going about their daily tasks. She had moved to Mexico several years earlier with her then-companion, the famous photographer Edward Weston, and decided to stay. She took many pictures of Mexican Indians and peasants that showed the dignity of her subjects and helped raise awareness of the social and economic divisions in Mexican society.

Modotti was a strong supporter of Communism. Like other Communists, she believed that land and other forms of wealth should be distributed equally among all members of a society. During this time, a vast divide existed between rich people and poor people in Mexico. A small number of very wealthy people owned most of the nation's farms and factories, while a huge number of workers and peasants struggled to get by with no land and little money or power. As Kahlo spent time with Modotti and her friends, she came to share their view that adopting Communist principles would help solve some of Mexico's social problems. She joined the Mexican Communist Party and began participating in meetings and protest marches.

Kahlo's interest in politics grew stronger in 1928, when President Álvaro Obregón was assassinated. Obregón was a popular leader who had first taken office eight years earlier, following the end of the Mexican Revolution. The Mexican government had made a number of positive changes under Obregón's leadership, including distributing land to poor people, increasing wages and rights for

Kahlo's younger sister, Christina, was the subject of Kahlo's painting
Woman in White, *which she painted in 1928. This was the same year*
that Kahlo again came into contact with Diego at a Communist meeting.

workers, and improving health care.

After Obregón's death, Kahlo and many of her friends hoped that José Vasconcelos—who had implemented many reforms as Obregón's minister of education—would become the new president. Instead, power passed to a group of leaders headed by

Plutarco Calles, who had been president before Obregón. Over the next few years, the Calles government took steps to reduce the power of the Catholic Church and limit people's religious freedom. It also resorted to threats and violence to silence its critics and political opponents, including members of the Communist Party.

Communism

In the years following her accident, Frida Kahlo became deeply committed to Communist political ideas. Communism is based on the belief that all people in a country should share equally in that country's property and wealth.

One of the first promoters of Communism was the German economist and philosopher Karl Marx, who outlined his political theories in two influential books, *The Communist Manifesto* (1848) and *Das Kapital* (1867). Marx argued that throughout history, the major countries of the world, like the United States, had been run under a system called capitalism. He explained that in a capitalist system, wealth and power tended to be concentrated in the hands of just a few people. Marx claimed that capitalism

was doomed to fail because ordinary working people would eventually rise up in revolt against the rich property owners in order to claim their own share of wealth and political power.

During World War I (1914-1918), followers of Marx's teachings started trying to put Communist governments in place in various countries. These activists encouraged peasants and workers to rise up against the wealthy ruling classes. In 1917, a group of revolutionaries led by Vladimir Lenin and Leon Trotsky succeeded in overthrowing Czar Nicholas II and installing a Communist government in Russia. Kahlo supported the principles of the Russian Revolution and became a member of the Mexican Communist Party.

Biological Truth of Feelings

Frida is the only example in the history of art of an artist who tore open her chest and heart to reveal the biological truth of her feelings.

Diego Rivera, quoted in Robin Richmond, *Painters and Places: Frida Kahlo in Mexico*. San Francisco: Pomegranate Artbooks, 1994, p. 84.

Meeting Diego Rivera

Through her association with the Mexican Communist Party, Kahlo once again came into contact with Diego Rivera. By this time, the respected mural artist had become one of the most famous people in all of Mexico. He was known not only for his artistic talent, but also for his Communist political views, outgoing personality, wild behavior, and numerous love affairs. Kahlo ran into Rivera at several Communist gatherings in 1928.

Determined to find out whether she was talented enough to make a living as a painter, Kahlo decided to show some of her paintings to Rivera and ask his opinion. One day, she visited him at the Ministry of Education Building in Mexico City, where he was working on a mural project. Knowing Rivera's reputation, she boldly declared, "I have not come to flirt, and even if you are a woman chaser, I have come to show you my paintings."[18]

Rivera remembered Kahlo as the young girl who had teased him as he worked on his mural at the National Preparatory School a few years earlier. Intrigued, he agreed to look at her paintings. Kahlo was excited when the prominent artist said that her work showed promise and encouraged her to continue painting. "The canvases revealed an unusual energy of expression," Rivera recalled. "They communicated a vital sensuality, complemented by a merciless yet sensitive power of observation. It was obvious to me that this girl was an authentic artist."[19]

Gets Married

Kahlo invited Rivera to come to the Blue House to see more of her paintings. Before long, their relationship evolved into a

Frida Kahlo and Diego Rivera in their garden. Their difficult marriage began on August 21, 1929, when they were wed in a civil ceremony in Mexico City.

romantic one. The muralist became a regular visitor at her home, and Kahlo often went to the Ministry of Education Building to watch him work. Rivera even used her as a model for a panel in his mural *Ballad of the Proletarian Revolution*. Kahlo appears as a revolutionary holding knives in one hand and a rifle in the other.

Kahlo's parents, especially her mother, did not approve of her relationship with Rivera. Although the muralist was wealthy and famous, he was also twenty years older than their daughter. They worried about his reputation for chasing pretty women, and the fact that his two previous marriages had ended in divorce. Finally, they felt that Frida and Diego made a very unlikely couple. He was tall, overweight, and homely, while Kahlo was short, petite, and attractive. Matilde Kahlo nicknamed the couple "the elephant and the dove."

Despite these concerns, however, Kahlo's parents reluctantly gave her permission to marry Rivera. They recognized that they could not afford to continue paying the medical bills from her accident. They also knew that Kahlo—with her independent spirit, fiery temper, and ongoing health problems—would be a handful for any husband. In fact, Guillermo Kahlo once warned Rivera that his daughter was "a devil," but the muralist simply replied, "I know it."[20]

Kahlo and Rivera were married on August 21, 1929, when she was twenty-two years old and he was forty-two. Because neither of them held strong religious beliefs, they had a civil ceremony rather than a church wedding. Kahlo wore a traditional Mexican blouse and skirt that she borrowed from her parents' maid. Ignoring the custom of the times, she chose to keep her maiden name. After the wedding, Kahlo moved out of the Blue House to live with her husband in an elegant home in the center of Mexico City.

From the beginning, the relationship between the two artists was a difficult and turbulent one. Although they shared a deep commitment to art and a passion for their Mexican homeland, they also shared an intense need for attention and a hot temper. Kahlo and Rivera loved each other, but they fought often and hurt each other many times by both having affairs. In fact, their marriage caused Kahlo so much pain that she once compared it to the effects of her accident. "I suffered two grave accidents in my life," she stated, "one in which a streetcar ran me over; the other accident is Diego."[21]

Chapter 3

Artistic Style Matures in the United States

Frida Kahlo had been married to painter Diego Rivera for just over a year when his work, combined with changes in Mexico's political climate, took them to the United States. Already struggling to adjust to her new life as the wife of a famous artist, Kahlo found that process even more difficult to handle in a foreign country. She spent three unhappy years in America, where her husband was always the center of attention and she was not taken seriously as an artist. Her feelings of homesickness were compounded by grief over a failed pregnancy and the death of her mother. The main benefit to Kahlo's time in the United States was that her unhappiness inspired her to develop her mature painting style.

Adjusts to Married Life

From the beginning of Kahlo's relationship with Rivera, it was clear that his top priority was his work. Shortly after their wedding, Rivera took on a huge project at the National Palace, where he painted a mural that depicted the entire history of Mexico. He also accepted a position as director of the

Kahlo painted The Bus *the year that she and Rivera were married. The painting shows how Kahlo was beginning to embrace her Mexican heritage in her artwork.*

prestigious San Carlos Art Academy, where he had studied as a young man. These demanding jobs kept him away from home most of the time.

Kahlo soon understood that if she wanted to spend time with her husband, she had to visit him at his mural site. She learned to cook his favorite meals and often brought his dinner to him at work. She spent many hours with him on the scaffold, talking with him and observing his technique. This experience influenced Kahlo's later paintings in a number of ways. Art historian Phyllis Tuchman explained:

> As she watched him paint, she learned the fundamentals of her craft. His imagery recurs in her pictures along with his palette—the sunbaked colors of pre-Columbian art. And from him—though his large-scale wall murals depict historical themes, and her small-

scale works relate her autobiography—she learned how to tell a story in paint.[22]

Rivera also influenced Kahlo in the early years of their relationship by turning her away from European art traditions and pointing her toward Mexican folk art traditions. One of the ways in which Kahlo demonstrated her interest in Mexican culture was by adopting a traditional style of dress. She began wearing a colorful Tehuana costume—similar to that worn by her Tehuantepec Indian ancestors—that featured a long, ruffled skirt, an embroidered blouse, and lots of jewelry.

Kahlo also started to incorporate elements of Mexican art and culture into her paintings following her marriage. In her 1929 Self-Portrait *Time Flies*, for instance, she appears wearing a simple cotton peasant blouse and pre-Conquest Mexican jewelry. She also stares directly at the viewer with a positive, determined expression. The main colors in the painting are green, white, and red—the colors of the Mexican flag. Biographer Hayden Herrera attributes the differences between this painting and *Self-Portrait in a Velvet Dress*, completed three years earlier, to Rivera's influence on Kahlo's self-image.

> She has replaced the luxurious Renaissance-style gown she wore in her first self-portrait with a cheap peasant blouse. No longer the winsome, melancholy aristocrat, she is now a contemporary Mexican girl possessed of all the candor and spunk she needed to lure Rivera down from his scaffold.[23]

Kahlo's Reality

Frida Kahlo did not paint her reality as it was seen, but as she felt it. The outside world is thereby reduced to its essentials, and a sequence of events condensed into a powerful climax.

Andrea Kettenmann, *Frida Kahlo: Pain and Passion*. Koln: Taschen, 2003, p. 35.

Political Changes in Mexico

Although Kahlo's paintings from this period project self-confidence, she was often overshadowed by her famous husband in the early years of their marriage. While he attracted a great deal of attention for his art and his political views, she stood by his side in her role as a devoted wife.

Just a few months after their wedding, Rivera had a falling out with the Mexican Communist Party. Many Communists were upset by the policies of the Calles government, which limited personal freedoms and favored wealthy property owners. They were ready to support an armed uprising to force Mexico to return to the democratic principles of the revolution. Rivera, however, did not believe that an armed uprising was a good idea. He argued that the Communists should try to work with the government to make necessary changes. Some members of the Mexican Communist Party claimed that Rivera was acting in his own self-interest rather than in the best interest of the Mexican people. They suggested that he supported the Calles government because he did not want to lose his job at the art academy or his commissions to paint murals in government buildings.

In the fall of 1929, this ongoing argument forced Rivera to resign from the Mexican Communist Party. Kahlo gave up her membership, too, as a show of support for her husband. Since many people in their circle of friends were fellow Communists, their decision led to a decline in their social life.

A short time later, Rivera accepted an invitation from Dwight W. Morrow, the U.S. ambassador to Mexico, to paint a mural at the Hernán Cortés Palace in Cuernavaca, about 50 miles south of Mexico City. Rivera accepted the commission, and Kahlo accompanied him to Cuernavaca. During their time there, she became pregnant. Her doctors warned her that the damage the accident had caused to her pelvis, spine, and reproductive organs could make it difficult or even dangerous for her to carry a baby. Rivera also made it clear that he was not interested in having another child, in addition to the three children he had already fathered in previous relationships. After considering these factors, Kahlo reluctantly decided to undergo an abortion. "We could not have a child," she recalled, "and I cried inconsolably but I distracted myself by cooking, dusting the house, sometimes by painting, and every day going to accompany Diego on the scaffold."[24]

As Rivera completed his mural in Cuernavaca, the political climate in Mexico continued to change in ways that were unfavorable to his career. First, the Calles government ended its sponsorship of mural projects. Then, as part of a campaign to silence political opponents, government officials arranged for Rivera to be fired from his job as director of the San Carlos Art Academy. Finding himself at odds with both the Calles government and the Mexican Communist Party, Rivera decided to accept an offer to paint murals in the United States.

Going to America

Kahlo was excited when she first learned of her husband's plan to travel to the United States. She had never been outside of Mexico before, and she looked forward to visiting American cities. Their trip was delayed for a while by the U.S. government, which initially denied them permission to enter the country because of their Communist political views. But a wealthy art patron, Albert Bender, was eventually able to arrange for the couple to receive entry visas through his network of government contacts.

After securing visas, Kahlo and Rivera arrived in California on November 10, 1930. Rivera fell in love with the United States right away. He was fascinated by the modern technology and architecture he saw in American cities. He also enjoyed being treated as a celebrity. A frequent guest at fancy restaurants and nightclubs in San Francisco, he attracted crowds of people with his outrageous stories and wild behavior.

Unfortunately for Kahlo, she did not share her husband's positive view of the United States. For one thing, she was disgusted by the extremes of wealth and poverty that she saw around her. Kahlo and Rivera had arrived in the United States in the early 1930s, during the Great Depression, a time of great economic hardship when many Americans lost their jobs, homes, and life savings. As she toured San Francisco, Kahlo could not help but notice the long lines of unemployed people waiting for a hot meal or a place to sleep. She thought about these people while she visited the luxu-

Kahlo and Rivera with some wealthy American patrons. People tended to view Kahlo as a quaint object next to the great artist Rivera.

rious homes of rich art patrons, ate at expensive restaurants, and attended parties at elegant art galleries. In a letter to a friend she wrote:

> I feel a bit of rage against all these rich guys here, since I have seen thousands of people in the most terrible misery without anything to eat and with no place to sleep. It is terrifying to see the rich having parties day and night while thousands of people are dying of hunger.[25]

While Rivera worked on his mural Allegory of California at the San Francisco Stock Exchange, Kahlo struggled with feelings of boredom and loneliness. She spent some of her time sketching and painting, but she found it difficult to take her work seriously when no one in the United States seemed to consider her an artist. Instead, people tended to view her as a quaint, decorative object that sometimes accompanied the great artist Diego Rivera. Photographer Edward Weston recalled that Kahlo looked like "a little doll alongside Diego"[26] as she toured the sights of San Francisco in her Tehuana outfits.

Another factor in Kahlo's unhappiness was that she experienced increasingly severe pain in her foot during this time. When the pain made it difficult for her to walk, she checked herself into San Francisco General Hospital. She was treated by a highly respected surgeon, Dr. Leo Eloesser, who became her lifelong friend and medical advisor.

Develops Her Mature Style

After her release from the hospital, Kahlo went back to painting and created some of the earliest works that show her mature style. For instance, she combined elements of reality and fantasy in her 1931 *Portrait of Luther Burbank*. Burbank was a scientist known for combining the genetic material of different plants to create unusual hybrids. Kahlo depicts Burbank as a hybrid— half man and half tree—with a trunk and roots instead of legs and feet. She shows him holding a growing plant in his hands, while his roots draw nourishment from a human skeleton buried under the ground. Some art critics believe she included this imagery to demonstrate her belief that all things are connected and exist in a cycle of life and death.

Kahlo continued painting in the spring of 1931, while her husband completed his *Allegory of California* mural and began working on a new project at the California School for Fine Arts. One of her best-known works from this period is a wedding portrait, *Frida and Diego Rivera*, which she presented as a gift to Albert Bender. In this painting, Kahlo appears in a colorful Tehuana costume. She looks small and frail next to her husband and rests one hand delicately on his. Rivera looks large and solid in a gray suit, and he

Kahlo's Portrait of Luther Burbank *combine elements of reality and fantasy.*

holds paintbrushes and a palette in one hand. Some art critics suggest that the painting reflects Kahlo's feelings of insignificance in her role as the adoring wife of the master artist.

As Rivera's second California mural neared completion, Kahlo looked forward to returning home to Mexico. The prospect of leaving the United States helped soften her feelings about the experience. "It did make sense to come here, because it opened my eyes and I have seen an enormous number of new and beautiful things,"[27] she declared. Toward the end of her visit, Kahlo began stepping out from her husband's shadow and exerting her independence. At parties and other events, she often drank alcohol, sang songs, flirted with men, and used profanity.

Kahlo was pleased to return to Mexico in June 1931. She and Rivera moved into the Blue House with her family while construction was completed on a new house in the fashionable San Ángel neighborhood of Mexico City. Rivera went back to work on his National Palace murals, and Kahlo settled back into her comfortable life at home.

Just a few months later, though, Kahlo learned that she would have to return to the United States. The prestigious Museum of Modern Art in New York City planned to honor Rivera with a special one-person exhibition of his works. The couple traveled to New York in November 1931, where they were once again greeted as celebrities and entertained at elegant receptions. When Rivera's show opened on December 22, the U.S. media described it as one of the biggest events of the year in the world of art.

Expresses Feelings of Anguish

The publicity surrounding Rivera's New York show led to a flood of invitations for him to paint murals in the United States. He accepted a commission to paint a mural celebrating technological progress at the Detroit Institute of Arts. In April 1932, Kahlo and her husband traveled to the Michigan city, which served as the capital of the American automobile industry. Rivera spent a great deal of time touring automobile factories and watching assembly lines in action. He loved the modern technology and featured it prominently in his *Detroit Industry* mural. Kahlo, on the other hand, found Detroit gloomy and boring.

During their stay in Michigan, Kahlo became pregnant again. She initially planned to have another abortion, but she eventually reconsidered and decided to try to have the baby. "At that time I was enthusiastic about having the child after having thought of all the difficulties that it would cause me,"[28] she wrote in her diary. Her husband supported her decision and encouraged her to follow her doctors' advice and spend as much time as possible resting in bed.

On July 4, 1932, Kahlo woke up bleeding heavily. She was taken by ambulance to Henry Ford Hospital, where she had a painful miscarriage. She spent two weeks in the hospital recovering. When she was released, Kahlo tried to appear upbeat in front of her husband and friends. In reality, though, she felt exhausted and depressed, and she expressed these feelings in her art.

Kahlo's anguish over her miscarriage inspired her to create some of her most personal and powerful paintings. *Henry Ford Hospital*, which she completed shortly after losing the baby, expresses her feelings about the tragic event. Kahlo depicts herself lying in a puddle of blood on an oversized hospital bed. She appears sad and lonely, with a single tear on her face. Surrounding the bed, and connected to her body by red lines resembling arteries, is a collection of objects that symbolize different aspects of her experience. The objects include a baby boy, a model of a female pelvis, a machine for sterilizing medical equipment, a snail, and a purple orchid. The bed appears to float in front of a desolate landscape of factories and smokestacks.

Kahlo Paints in Detroit

Frida began work on a series of masterpieces which had no precedent in the history of art—paintings which exalted the feminine qualities of endurance of truth, reality, cruelty, and suffering. Never before had a woman put such agonized poetry on canvas as Frida did at this time in Detroit.

Diego Rivera, *My Art, My Life*. New York: Citadel, 1960, p. 123-24.

Some art critics contend that *Henry Ford Hospital* marked the emergence of Kahlo's mature painting style. Like many of her later works, it incorporates many symbols that work together to tell a story. It was also the first time that Kahlo painted on a sheet of metal. She was probably inspired to do this by a Mexican folk art tradition known as retablo, or ex-voto, painting. These small paintings on pieces of tin often decorated the walls of churches in Mexico. Each painting told the story of a person's misfortune, such as an accident or an illness, and included a dedication thanking God or a particular saint for helping the person overcome it. Kahlo collected retablos and often used elements of this style in her later works.

Loses Her Mother

In September 1932, just two months after suffering a miscarriage, Kahlo received a telegram informing her that her mother was dying of cancer. She made the difficult five-day train journey to Mexico City and arrived in time to see her mother for a few days before she died. Kahlo stayed in Mexico for a month to help her father, then returned to her husband in Detroit.

Self-Portrait on the Border Line Between Mexico and the United States *reflects what Kahlo saw as the contrast between the cultures of the two countries.*

Kahlo's grief over her mother's death inspired her to create one of her most disturbing paintings, *My Birth*. In this work the mother who is giving birth to Kahlo is apparently dead, because she has a sheet pulled over her head. On the wall above the bed, a portrait of the Virgin of Sorrows looks down on the tragic scene in anguish. Art critic Robin Richmond argued that the painting expresses Kahlo's grief over the near-simultaneous loss of her baby and her mother. "The covered body is both Frida and her mother, Matilde," she noted. "It is a picture about the loss of self—of child and of parent simultaneously. What greater grief can there be?"[29]

Kahlo continued painting during the remaining five months that she and her husband spent in Detroit. A work that clearly expresses her feelings of homesickness during that period is *Self-Portrait on the Border Line between Mexico and the United States*. Wearing a ruffled pink gown and lace gloves, Kahlo stands in the center of the painting. She holds a small Mexican flag in one hand and a cigarette in the other. On one side she presents her view of Mexico: a natural world in which the sun and moon look down over an ancient Aztec pyramid, fertility statues, and growing vegetables and flowers. On the other side she presents a contrasting view of the United States: an industrial landscape full of lifeless skyscrapers, factories filling the sky with smoke, and machines rooted into the earth.

Art critics have interpreted this 1932 work as an expression of Kahlo's dislike for the United States, and what she saw as its artificial, mechanized culture. They claim that the painting emphasizes the contrast between this culture and that of Kahlo's homeland, which she viewed as steeped in history and connections to the natural world. Even as she turned out paintings that would eventually be considered among her best, however, Kahlo received little recognition or respect as an artist during her stay in the United States. In fact, the *Detroit News* printed an article that dismissed her efforts with the headline "Wife of the Master Mural Painter Gleefully Dabbles in Works of Art."

Faces Controversy in New York

Despite Kahlo's feelings of unhappiness about living in the United States, her husband was not interested in returning to Mexico. When Rivera received an invitation to paint a mural in

Kahlo's Distinctive Style

When Frida Kahlo became romantically involved with Diego Rivera, she adopted a new style of dress that celebrated her Mexican identity. She wore colorful, decorative Tehuana costumes from the Tehuantepec region of southwestern Mexico. Some of Kahlo's Indian ancestors on her mother's side came from this region, where strong women traditionally played a dominant role in society.

Kahlo enjoyed wearing the Tehuana costume to please her husband, to showcase Mexican culture, and to feel closer to the indigenous people of Mexico. Her distinctive clothing made her "a style legend in her lifetime," according to Georgina Howell in *Harper's Bazaar*. "On almost every day of her life, she dressed as if she were going to a fiesta."

The Tehuana costume consists of long, full skirts covered with ruffles, lace, and ribbons; embroidered cotton peasant blouses; lots of ornate pre-Conquest jewelry; and braided hair decorated with ribbons, flowers, or scarves and arranged on top of the head. Kahlo was one of the first prominent Mexican women to adopt this flamboyant style of dress, but many others soon followed her lead. "In the twenties and thirties Tehuana costume was adopted by many educated Mexican city women," Andrea Kettenmann explained in *Frida Kahlo: Pain and Passion*. "It perfectly matched the growing spirit of nationalism and the revived interest in Indian culture."

Georgina Howell, "Frida Kahlo," *Harper's Bazaar*, November 2001, p. 234; Andrea Kettenmann, *Frida Kahlo: Pain and Passion*. Koln: Taschen, 2003, p. 26.

Kahlo wore the Tehuana costume to celebrate her Mexican identity.

the lobby of the RCA Building in Rockefeller Center, he eagerly accepted the commission. Kahlo dutifully accompanied him to New York City in March 1933.

Rivera spent the next several months working on his Rockefeller Center mural, titled *Man at the Crossroads Looking with Hope and High Vision to the Choosing of a New and Better Future*. In the meantime, Kahlo did not do much painting because she found it difficult to concentrate in New York City. She tried to forget her troubles by developing an active social life. She went to movies, parties, and concerts, and she shopped for designer clothes to replace her famous Tehuana costumes.

One of the paintings that Kahlo did complete during this time, *My Dress Hangs There or New York, 1933*, shows that she still felt a strong desire to return to Mexico. Unlike most of her other works, this painting does not include a portrait of Kahlo. Instead, one of her dresses hangs empty in the center of the scene. It is suspended from a ribbon that is strung between a toilet and a trophy. The scene behind the dress includes many images that Kahlo associated with New York, including skyscrapers, factories, gasoline pumps, a telephone, a full garbage can, and the sexy actress Mae West. The foreground is a collage of newspaper clippings that picture crowds of hungry people standing in bread lines.

Some art critics claim that this painting represents the starkly differing views of New York City held by Kahlo and Rivera. It includes symbols of money and modern industry, which held a great deal of appeal for Rivera. In contrast, it also includes symbols of social problems and declining moral values, which were very disturbing to Kahlo. In her work, however, Kahlo seems to have the final say about whether she and her husband should return home. Since Kahlo is absent from the painting, it implies that she has already left for Mexico—perhaps on the steamship that can be seen in the distance leaving New York Harbor.

Kahlo and her husband finally did leave the United States in December 1933, following a heated controversy over the content and themes included in Rivera's *Man at the Crossroads* mural. Rivera upset his wealthy patrons, the Rockefeller family, by featuring a portrait of Russian Communist leader Vladimir Lenin in the mural. The Rockefellers demanded that he paint over it, but he refused. In response, they fired Rivera and ordered that his painting be covered up. Both Rivera and Kahlo were outraged by this turn of events. They believed that artists should have the freedom to express their views, even if those views were controversial. But the Rockefellers, who had earned their wealth through business, felt that they should not have to pay for a painting that contradicted their views, or that went against the governing principles of the United States, meaning capitalism. So Kahlo and her husband, dejected and running out of money, went home to Mexico.

Chapter 4

Paintings Chronicle Her Turbulent Marriage

During the 1930s and 1940s, Frida Kahlo started to move out of her famous husband's shadow and gain recognition for her own work as an artist. She created some of her most intense and powerful paintings during this period. Unfortunately for Kahlo, the inspiration for many of these works came from her troubled marriage to Diego Rivera.

The Ultimate Betrayal

Upon their return from the United States in 1934, Kahlo and Rivera finally moved into their new home in the San Ángel neighborhood of Mexico City. Designed by their good friend, the architect Juan O'Gorman, it consisted of two separate structures: a large pink house for Rivera; and a smaller blue house for Kahlo. The two houses shared a garden courtyard and were connected by a second-story walkway. The idea behind the unique design was to give both artists space to work individually. But the home also reflected the turbulent nature of Kahlo and Rivera's relationship, which featured periods of intimate connection as well as periods of pain and separation.

Kahlo decorated her house in a style that reflected her love for Mexican history and culture. She used bright colors and included many pieces of traditional Mexican folk art. Her kitchen and dining room, for instance, had a yellow floor covered with straw mats and shelves full of decorative clay pots. Kahlo also filled her house with an assortment of unusual pets, including parrots, spider monkeys, and a fawn. She allowed her beloved animals to run loose in the house and courtyard, where they often amused guests.

Although Kahlo and Rivera enjoyed their new home, their return to Mexico marked the beginning of a particularly difficult time in their marriage. Rivera had loved the United States, and he had found his time there to be very exciting. Back in Mexico, on the other hand, he felt bored and unhappy. In February 1934, when Rivera learned that his controversial *Man at the Crossroads* mural at Rockefeller Center in New York City had been destroyed, he grew angry and depressed. He blamed Kahlo for these feelings, because she had disliked the United States and insisted that they return home.

Partly as a way to punish his wife, Rivera entered into an affair with her younger sister, Cristina. Since Cristina was the most important person in Kahlo's life other than Rivera, Kahlo viewed their affair as the ultimate betrayal. She was emotionally devastated by it, and it took a toll on her health. Meanwhile, the effects of polio and the trolley accident continued to cast shadows over her life. She ended up being hospitalized three times in 1934. On one of these occasions, she had several toes amputated in an attempt to relieve the pain in her right foot.

After learning of the affair, Kahlo moved out of the San Ángel home she had shared with Rivera. She lived in an apartment in Mexico City for a while, and she also made an extended trip to New York City to visit friends. During this time, Kahlo made the difficult decision to forgive her sister and reconcile with her husband. She sent Rivera a letter from New York expressing her continued love for him and her willingness to accept his infidelity. "I love you more than my own skin, and … though you may not love me in the same way, you still love me somewhat, isn't that so?" she wrote. "I shall always hope that that continues, and with that I am content."[30]

Paintings Are Her Memoirs

Kahlo's art is to painting what the memoir is to literature—self-absorbed, confessional, and hard to dismiss as a flash in the pan.

Stephanie Mencimer, "The Trouble with Frida Kahlo," *Washington Monthly*, June 2002, p. 26

Turning Pain into Art

Even though Kahlo eventually forgave Rivera and moved back into their home, she continued to struggle with the emotional devastation that his affair with her sister had caused. She dealt with her feelings of hurt and betrayal by expressing them in her art. During their separation, and over the next few years, she produced a number of paintings that seem to refer to this painful episode in her life.

In 1935, for instance, Kahlo painted one of her most violent and disturbing works, *A Few Small Nips*. Kahlo once said that she was inspired to paint this picture by reading a newspaper story about a man who had murdered his lover. When the man was arrested and charged with the crime, he protested to the authorities, "But I only gave her a few small nips!" Despite the connection to this incident, however, many art critics believe that Kahlo painted this picture in reference to the emotional wounds Rivera inflicted on her by having an affair with her sister.

In 1937, Kahlo produced another powerful image based on her troubled relationship with Rivera, titled *Memory or The Heart*. This self-portrait shows Kahlo standing in the center of the frame, with one foot on land and the other in water. She wears European clothing and has short hair, and there are tears running down her cheeks. A hole in her chest is bisected by a long pole, with a tiny Cupid balancing on each end. An enormous heart lies at her feet, spurting blood onto the ground. Kahlo is pictured between two dresses that represent her former selves: a schoolgirl's uniform and a Tehuana costume. Kahlo has no arms, but each otherwise empty dress contains an arm that reaches toward her.

The painting makes it clear that Kahlo's heart, or romantic life, is the source of considerable pain. Whenever she separated from

Memory or The Heart *is one of several paintings that show Kahlo's great emotional pain based on her troubled relationship with Rivera.*

Rivera, she stopped wearing the fancy Tehuana dresses that he loved and cut off her long hair. Art critics have interpreted the fact that Kahlo pictured herself without arms to mean that she felt helpless to change her situation. "*Memory* is as simple and direct as a valentine," noted biographer Hayden Herrera. "Torn from her body, Frida's huge heart lies at her feet pumping rivers of blood into the landscape…. The greater the pain she wished to convey—especially pain caused by rejection from Diego—the bloodier Frida's self-portraits became."[31]

Welcomes Trotsky to Mexico

Throughout these difficult years in their relationship, both Kahlo and Rivera remained deeply committed to Communist political ideas. In 1937, they helped convince the Mexican government to allow Leon Trotsky to enter the country. Trotsky was one of the leaders of the 1917 Russian Revolution, which succeeded in overthrowing Czar Nicholas II and installing a Communist government in Russia. For the next few years, Trotsky served as a diplomat and general under fellow Communist leader Vladimir Lenin.

When Lenin died in 1924, Joseph Stalin moved quickly to take his place as head of the newly formed Soviet Union. Stalin turned out to be one of the most brutal and ruthless dictators of the twentieth century. Over the course of his twenty-five-year reign, he murdered or imprisoned millions of his own people in order to maintain his grip on power. As one of Stalin's political opponents, Trotsky faced extreme danger. He left the Soviet Union in 1928 and spent the next several years moving from country to country in Europe and criticizing Stalin's government.

Recognizing the threat that Stalin's agents posed to Trotsky's life, Rivera and Kahlo arranged for him and his wife, Natalia, to come to Mexico. The Trotskys moved into Kahlo's family home, the Blue House, which was outfitted with bodyguards and other security measures for their protection. At first, Kahlo and Rivera spent a great deal of time with the Communist revolutionary, whom they admired greatly.

Many biographers claim that Kahlo had an affair with Trotsky, although others doubt that this could have occurred, given the tight security surrounding the much older man. In any case, Kahlo painted a full-length self-portrait dedicated to Trotsky. She presented it to him on his birthday, November 7, the year he arrived in Mexico. In this work, Kahlo appears very calm and dignified in

Kahlo going to meet Leon Trotsky and his wife as they arrive in Mexico in 1937.

a formal gown and shawl. She holds a bouquet of flowers in one hand and a handwritten note in the other. The note says that the she gives the picture to Trotsky "with all love."

The close friendship between the Trotskys and their hosts did not last long. Partly due to the appearance of intimacy between Kahlo and Trotsky, and partly because the two couples had different social styles and political views, they soon went their separate ways. Trotsky and his wife moved out of the Blue House in 1939, and the following year he was murdered by one of Stalin's supporters. Kahlo then embraced Stalin and turned against Trotsky, claiming that the late Communist leader had "irritated me from the time he arrived … because he thought he was a big deal."[32]

Surrealism

Surrealism is an artistic movement that was founded by the French poet André Breton in Paris in 1924. In the *Manifesto of Surrealism* he published that year, Breton described Surrealism as a way to express "the real functioning of thought ... in the absence of all control exercised by reason." Surrealist writers and artists tried to represent the innermost thoughts and feelings of the subconscious mind in their work. These works often present a bizarre or distorted version of reality that resembles a strange dream. One of the best-known Surrealist painters is Salvador Dali (1904-1989).

Upon visiting Mexico in 1938, Breton discovered that Kahlo's paintings included some Surrealist elements. He tried to adopt Kahlo as a Surrealist, but she denied any connection with the artistic movement. "Breton thought I was a Surrealist but I wasn't," she declared in *Harper's Bazaar*. "I never painted dreams. I painted my own reality." Nevertheless, Breton's attention helped Kahlo gain greater recognition in the art world.

In the years since Kahlo's death, art critics have generally agreed that her paintings should not be associated with the Surrealist movement. "Her work differs from Surrealism in that her fantasy was always rooted in concrete fact and immediate experience," Hayden Herrera wrote in *Frida Kahlo: The Paintings*. "Frida did not want to mystify. She wanted to communicate her feelings with the greatest possible clarity and directness."

Andre Breton, *Manifestoes of Surrealism*, translated from the French by Richard Seaver and Helen R. Lane. Ann Arbor: University of Michigan Press, 1969; Hayden Herrera, *Frida Kahlo: The Paintings*. New York: HarperCollins, 1991, p. 124; Georgina Howell, "Frida Kahlo," *Harper's Bazaar*, November 2001, p. 234.

Gains Recognition

In 1938, while Kahlo and Rivera were hosting the Trotskys in the Blue House, they received another prominent visitor into their social circle. André Breton, the French poet and critic who founded the artistic movement known as Surrealism, came to Mexico with his wife, Jacqueline. Kahlo and Rivera were more than happy to entertain them, and the two couples became good friends.

As soon as Breton saw Kahlo's paintings, he fell in love with them. He especially liked the bizarre, dreamlike imagery that she included in some of her self-portraits. He claimed that this sort of imagery connected Kahlo's work to his Surrealist movement. But Kahlo did not consider herself a Surrealist. Unlike the European painters associated with this artistic movement, she painted her conscious feelings and experiences rather than her subconscious thoughts and dreams. Nevertheless, Kahlo felt pleased that such a prominent art critic had taken an interest in her work.

Kahlo's spirits received another boost that year when she sold her first paintings. Before this time, she had painted mainly for herself, as a way to express and cope with her feelings. Although she had given away many paintings to friends and supporters, she remained relatively unknown among wealthy art collectors. This situation started to change in 1938, when the American actor Edward G. Robinson visited Mexico and bought four of her works for his collection at $200 each. For Kahlo, the sale provided some valuable financial independence. "For me it was such a surprise," she acknowledged. "I marveled and said: 'This way I am going to be able to be free, I'll be able to travel and do what I want without asking Diego for money."[33]

A short time later, Kahlo received an invitation to show her paintings at the Julien Levy Gallery in New York City. Although this respected gallery was best known for promoting the work of Surrealists, Kahlo welcomed the opportunity to hold her first solo exhibition there. Breton offered to write the introduction to the catalog for the show. In describing the twenty-five paintings featured, he famously compared Kahlo's work to "a ribbon around a bomb."[34]

Kahlo's show at the Julien Levy Gallery attracted many of Rivera's celebrity friends and was considered a success. "The flutter of the week in Manhattan was caused by the first exhibition of paintings by famed muralist Diego Rivera's wife, Frida Kahlo," noted a reviewer for *Time* magazine. "Frida's pictures, mostly painted in oil on copper, had the daintiness of miniatures, the vivid reds and yellows of Mexican tradition, the playfully bloody fancy of an unsentimental child."[35]

The success of Kahlo's New York show led to an invitation from

Breton to exhibit her works in Paris. Kahlo accepted the invitation and sailed to France in early 1939. Although she was excited to see Europe, Kahlo did not enjoy her visit. She felt somewhat alarmed by the tense atmosphere she encountered there in the months before the start of World War II. She also disliked the way that

Kahlo's The Frame *became the first work by a twentieth-century Mexican artist to be purchased by the prestigious Louvre museum in Paris, France.*

her seventeen paintings were displayed alongside what she called "junk" from Mexico—including photographs, retablo paintings and other popular art, and pre-Conquest sculptures.

Even though Kahlo was unhappy with the arrangement of the Paris show, the exposure helped her earn the admiration of several of Europe's most famous artists, including Pablo Picasso and Wassily Kandinsky. At the end of the exhibition, the prestigious Louvre museum purchased one of her paintings for its permanent collection. The museum selected a 1938 work called *The Frame,* which is a self-portrait that Kahlo overlaid with a clear glass frame painted with colorful flowers and birds. *The Frame* was the first work by a twentieth-century Mexican artist to be purchased by the Louvre. Back in Mexico, Rivera boasted about his wife's success to everyone he met.

Torn Apart by Divorce

Kahlo left Paris in the spring of 1939. Her successful exhibitions had marked a high point in her career as an artist, and she returned to Mexico feeling happy and confident. Unfortunately for Kahlo, these feelings did not last long. She came home to find her husband deeply involved with another woman and determined to end their marriage. Although Kahlo was shocked and hurt by his decision, Rivera insisted that he was acting in his wife's best interests by filing for divorce. "I believe that with my decision I am helping Frida's life to develop in the best possible way," he stated. "She is young and beautiful. She has had much success in the most demanding art centers. She has every possibility that life can offer her, while I am already old and no longer have much to offer her."[36]

Kahlo's divorce from Rivera was finalized on November 6, 1939. She completed one of her most famous paintings, *The Two Fridas*, on that day. In this work—her first large canvas—Kahlo included not one, but two images of herself. The self-portrait on the left shows Kahlo wearing a white, lacy, high-collared dress in a European style. The self-portrait on the right shows her wearing a colorful dress in the style of the Indians of Mexico. Some critics claim that Kahlo intended for these two versions of herself to represent her mestiza (mixed Spanish and Indian) ancestry.

Kahlo painted The Two Fridas *as a result of her divorce from Rivera.*

The two Fridas sit together on a wicker bench holding hands. Both of their hearts are visible inside their chests, and the two hearts are connected by the blood flowing through a long vein. The Spanish Frida's heart appears to be sliced open, and she holds a clamp on a vein in an unsuccessful effort to stop the flow of blood. The Indian Frida's heart is whole, but it is connected to a tiny portrait of Diego Rivera as a little boy that she holds in her lap. Both Fridas stare at the viewer with a serious expression, although the Spanish Frida appears much paler and less healthy than the Indian Frida.

In discussing this painting, Kahlo once said that one version of herself represents the Frida that Rivera loved, and the other version of herself is the Frida that he no longer loved. Some critics have interpreted *The Two Fridas* as a visual representation of Kahlo's feelings during her divorce. They claim that one part of her probably felt weak and vulnerable, as if the emotional pain might be too much for her to bear, while another part of her felt determined to survive the breakup of her marriage.

Art critic and Kahlo biographer Hayden Herrera argues that *The Two Fridas* simply presents the two sides of Kahlo's personality—the divided nature that many people who knew her felt. "There was the flamboyant creature whom she presented to the world, the woman full of laughter, compassion, and heroic strength…" Herrera wrote. "This persona hid the dark side of Frida, the needy, manipulating woman who in part embraced the role of victim in order to be admired for her martyrdom."[37]

Pain Reflected in Art

During her divorce, Kahlo painted more intensively than she ever had before. She painted partly as a way to earn money, because she wanted to be financially independent. But she also painted as a way to express and cope with her feelings of anger and sorrow. Some critics believe that Kahlo did some of her best work during this painful time in her life, even though many of the paintings have a darker, angrier quality than her earlier work. "The self-portraits from the divorce period are no longer pretty, folkloric, or charming," Herrera explained. "They are full of repressed rage, and Frida's tearless face has been hardened into an accusing mask."[38]

An example of a painting that shows Kahlo's feelings of anger and frustration toward Rivera during their divorce is 1940's *Self-Portrait with Cropped Hair*. In this work, Kahlo sits in a chair wearing a dark-gray man's suit that is several sizes too big for her. Her hair has been cut short in a masculine style, and her formerly long locks are strewn all over the chair and the floor. Kahlo holds a pair of scissors in her lap, with the sharp ends open and pointing toward herself. At the top of the scene are some musical notes and lyrics that read: "Look, if I loved you, it was for your hair. Now that you are bald, I do not love you anymore."

Kahlo's Self-Portrait with Cropped Hair *shows her feelings toward Rivera during their divorce.*

Critics have pointed out that Kahlo appears to be wearing Rivera's suit in the picture. Some suggested that the scissors pointing toward her in the painting may symbolize her desire to take revenge for her husband's betrayal of her. Both Kahlo and Rivera loved her long hair and considered it an important part of her feminine beauty. In this way, cutting off her hair served to punish Rivera and also showed how the divorce made Kahlo question her self-image.

Kahlo Reflects on Marriage

Being the wife of Diego is the most marvelous thing in the world.... Diego is not anybody's husband and never will be, but he is a great comrade.

Frida Kahlo, quoted in Robin Richmond, *Painters and Places: Frida Kahlo in Mexico*. San Francisco: Pomegranate Artbooks, 1994, p. 67.

Reconciles with Rivera

The paintings Kahlo completed during her divorce from Rivera clearly express her pain and anger. These feelings also prompted her to consume large amounts of alcohol, which took a toll on her already fragile health. In the fall of 1940, her longtime friend and advisor, Dr. Leo Eloesser, convinced her to come to California for medical treatment. Seeing the extent of Kahlo's unhappiness, Eloesser encouraged her to reconcile with Rivera. He recommended that Kahlo forgive her husband and learn to accept his infidelities, because he felt that the divorce had been bad for her health. "Diego loves you very much, and you love him," the doctor told Kahlo. "It is also the case, and you know it better than I, that besides you, he has two great loves: 1) painting, 2) women in general. He has never been, nor ever will be, monogamous [fully committed to one person]."[39]

Kahlo soon encountered Rivera in San Francisco, where he was painting a mural. The two artists acknowledged that they had missed each other, and they decided to reconcile. Before Kahlo agreed to marry Rivera again, however, she laid out several conditions. As Rivera recalled in his autobiography, Kahlo insisted that

> She would provide for herself financially from the proceeds of her own work; that I would pay half of our household expenses—nothing more.... She [also] said that, with the images of all my other women flashing through her mind, she couldn't possibly

make love with me…. I was so happy to have Frida back that I assented to everything.[40]

Kahlo married Rivera for the second time on December 8, 1940, in San Francisco. Upon returning to Mexico a few months later, they moved into the Blue House together. The two San Ángel houses served as their studios. Although Rivera continued to have affairs with other women, for the most part Kahlo managed to accept his behavior. "The remarriage functions well," she wrote Eloesser six months later. "Better mutual understanding and on my part, fewer investigations of the tedious kind, with respect to other women."[41]

As Kahlo changed her attitude about her husband's affairs, she also entered into romantic relationships of her own, with both men and women. "They had reached a period of mature accommodation," noted one biographer. "Frida would tease him now about his [affairs], rather than crumble into despair. She had other fish to fry. She had friends and lovers. Diego, too, was a cherished friend now, and sometime husband, but no longer the intense focus of her innocent, youthful dreams."[42]

Kahlo expressed her changed feelings about her relationship with Rivera in her art work from this period. In the 1941 painting *Self-Portrait with Braid*, for instance, she appears to be wearing the hair she cut off a year earlier in *Self-Portrait with Cropped Hair*. Although the elaborate braid on top of her head seems to represent the return of her femininity, Kahlo also stands among sharp leaves and wears a necklace that looks heavy and uncomfortable. Some critics claimed that the details in this picture suggest Kahlo approached her remarriage with more realistic expectations of what life with Rivera would be like.

Chapter 5

Art Reflects Kahlo's Declining Health

I n the mid-1940s, Kahlo's health began to decline steadily. She endured a number of surgeries on her back and leg, spent a great deal of her time in bed, and turned to drugs and alcohol for relief from her severe pain. Her paintings from the last decade of her life express her alternating feelings of helplessness and determination in the face of physical and emotional suffering.

Sharing Her Gifts

In the years following her remarriage to Diego Rivera, Kahlo found several new outlets for her artistic gifts. In 1942, she started keeping a diary, which she filled with memories of her childhood, thoughts about her life and career, and sketches of ideas for new paintings. Kahlo was also elected to serve as a member of the Seminario de Cultura Mexicana, an organization that promoted Mexican art and culture.

In 1943, Kahlo began teaching art classes at the School of

Kahlo working in her studio. In the years after remarrying Rivera, Kahlo concentrated on several new artistic outlets.

Painting and Sculpture in Mexico City. Most of her students were teenagers from poor and working-class families. Rather than following conventional techniques and having them paint lifeless objects in the classroom, she encouraged her students to paint scenes that held meaning in their lives.

Kahlo gave her students lessons in Mexican history and culture by taking them to visit ancient ruins, Catholic churches, and the bustling streets and colorful marketplaces of Mexico City. Kahlo's unusual teaching methods made her classes very popular. Over the next few years, though, she was forced to limit her teaching schedule as her health declined. Four of her best students continued their lessons privately at the Blue House. Known as Los Fridos, this group remained devoted to Kahlo for the remainder of her life.

Happy To Be Alive

I am not sick. I am broken. But I am happy to be alive as long as I can paint.

Frida Kahlo, quoted in Hayden Herrera, *Frida Kahlo: The Paintings*. New York: HarperCollins, 1991, p. 211.

Struggling with Failing Health

By the mid-1940s, Kahlo's back pain had become so severe that she was often confined to her bed. She tried a number of treatments to support or improve the alignment of her spine, including wearing braces made of leather, steel, and plaster. In order to distract herself and her visitors from the braces, she often decorated them with drawings, flowers, feathers, stickers, mirrors, and political messages.

As her health failed and she increasingly found herself stuck in bed, Kahlo began to undertake more still-life paintings of arranged objects. Some critics saw striking similarities between these paintings and her self-portraits. Kahlo often painted bruised and damaged fruit, for instance, which the critics claimed represented her battered emotions and deteriorating body.

Kahlo also continued to paint self-portraits that explicitly depict her pain and suffering. One such work is *The Broken Column*, which she completed in 1944, during a five-month period when she had to wear a steel brace to support her back. This self-portrait shows Kahlo nude, with a brace strapped around her torso, standing in front of a bleak landscape full of deep ravines. The middle of her body is torn open to reveal a crumbling marble column where the vertebrae of her spine should be. She has sharp nails sticking out of her face and body, and tears are streaming down her face.

Although Kahlo seems to present herself as the tragic victim of a broken body in this picture, she insisted that this was not the whole story. As she pointed out to one of her students, her eyes are twinkling in the painting, and her pupils are tiny doves of peace. She described these details as "my little joke on pain and suffering, and your pity."[43] In some ways, Kahlo seemed to gain strength and courage by exposing her pain to the world. "Now more than ever, painting was a weapon for survival," biographer Hayden Herrera

Kahlo painted Flower of Life *in 1944, a period when her health began to decline.*

noted. "Determined to confront and communicate her predicament, she painted herself as the heroic sufferer."[44]

In 1946, Kahlo traveled to New York City to undergo major back surgery. The operation involved fusing together four vertebrae in her spine and inserting a metal rod to hold them in place. She spent two months recovering in the hospital, and during this time she became dependent on morphine to help her deal with the intense pain. "This medication is so marvelous," she wrote to her old friend Alejandro Gómez Arias, "and my body is so full of vitality, that they put me on my poor feet today for two minutes, and I myself don't believe it."[45]

Unfortunately for Kahlo, the operation was not successful. Wracked by severe pain, she became increasingly dependent on the numbing effects of drugs and alcohol. Kahlo expressed her pain and desperation in the 1946 painting *The Little Deer*. In this work, she places her own head on the body of an antlered buck. The deer's body has been pierced by nine arrows, and it runs desperate and bleeding through a forest during a thunderstorm. Some critics claim that Kahlo intended for this picture to convey the severity of her pain and to acknowledge the possibility of her death.

Quality of Work Declines

When Kahlo returned to Mexico following her surgery, Rivera initially spent a lot of time at her bedside taking care of her. She enjoyed being the center of her husband's attention for a change, since usually she had to compete with his work, his admirers, and his mistresses. Some biographers claim that Kahlo may have occasionally used her poor health as a way to get attention. They note that she often seemed to fall ill or schedule elective surgeries at times when Rivera was occupied with a major project or another woman. Even her longtime friend, Dr. Leo Eloesser, expressed the opinion that some of her surgeries may not have been medically necessary. Similarly, biographer Hayden Herrera pointed out that "if Frida's physical problems had been as grave as she made out, she would never have been able to translate them into art."[46]

By the 1950s, however, Kahlo's health declined to the point that it affected her work. After undergoing several more operations on her spine in 1950, Kahlo got a serious infection that forced her to spend nearly a year in the hospital. Rivera tried to make her feel at home by decorating her room with flowers, toys, and other gifts. Kahlo received many visitors at her bedside, and she always managed to dress up in colorful outfits, braid her hair, and put on makeup. Friends and relatives remember that she kept her sense of humor and entertained them with stories, jokes, and puppet

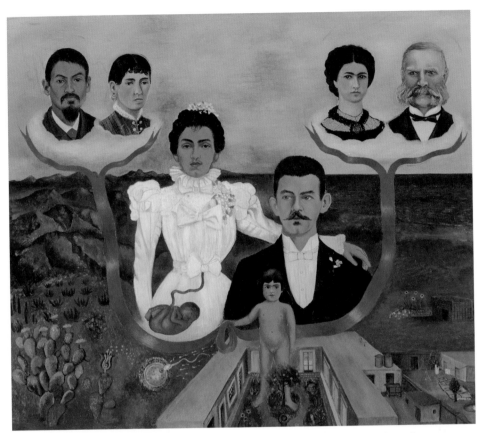

Unlike her previous works, My Family, *lacked the extreme technical precision for which Kahlo had become famous.*

shows. But Kahlo was only able to make these efforts with the help of very strong painkillers.

When Kahlo was finally released from the hospital, Rivera encouraged her to tell the story of her family background and personal history in a series of paintings. She obliged by painting *My Family*, a work that features portraits of her parents, grandparents, and sisters. Like other paintings from this period, however, it shows the effects of her increasing pain, weakness, and addiction to painkillers. One biographer wrote:

> Whereas her work up to 1951 had been executed with extreme technical precision, in what might almost be called miniaturist style, the poor state of her health now

began to affect the steadiness of her hand. After 1951 she was in such severe pain that she was no longer able to work without taking painkillers. Her increasingly strong medication must be seen as the reason for the looser, hastier, almost careless brushwork, thicker application of paint, and less precise execution of detail which now began to characterize her painting.[47]

Takes a Curtain Call

In April 1953, Kahlo's paintings finally appeared in a solo exhibition in her native Mexico. At first the show was scheduled to take place at the National Institute for Fine Arts, which was a tremendous honor for any Mexican artist. Unfortunately for Kahlo, by this time her health was too poor for her to participate

Kahlo's Personal Invitation

During her lifetime, Frida Kahlo witnessed only one solo exhibition of her works in her native Mexico. It took place a year before her death, on April 13, 1953, in the gallery of her friend Lola Alvarez Bravo in Mexico City. Kahlo sent out handwritten invitations to the event that included the following poem:

With friendship and affection
Coming straight from the heart
It gives me pleasure to invite you
To this exposition of my art....

I only want you to give me
Your opinion sincere and fine;
You pose as being learned,
So let your knowledge shine.

These canvases I've painted
I did with my own hands;
They wait for you upon the walls
To please you as I planned.

That is enough, my dearest pal:
With friendship deep and true,
Frida Kahlo de Rivera
Sends heartfelt thanks to you.

Raquel Tibol, *Frida Kahlo: An Open Life*. Translated by Elinor Randall. Albuquerque: University of New Mexico Press, 1993, p. 154.

in an opening at the major national museum. Instead, her good friend Lola Alvarez Bravo arranged to hold the exhibition at her Galería Arte Contemporáneo (Gallery of Contemporary Art) in Mexico City.

As the April 13 date of the opening approached, it appeared that Kahlo would be too sick to attend. She could no longer walk, and her doctors forbade her to leave her bed. Determined to enjoy the greatest moment of her career as an artist, however, Kahlo arranged for her four-poster bed and canopy to be delivered to the gallery and set up in the midst of her paintings. She also sent the mirror that she used to paint self-portraits and many of the decorations from her bedroom.

On the evening of the show, Kahlo arrived in an ambulance with a motorcycle escort. She was carried into the gallery on a stretcher and placed dramatically on her bed. Friends and admirers lined up to greet and congratulate her as she lay there. Kahlo even joined in the festivities by sipping cocktails and singing songs. "She had never been braver nor more stylish," noted one biographer. "It was a celebration of her life as much as of her art, and she knew it."[48]

The highly successful exhibition turned out to be Kahlo's final triumph, as her health continued to deteriorate. In July 1953, doctors discovered that her painful right leg had become infected with gangrene. They soon decided that they had no choice but to amputate her leg at the knee. Kahlo initially viewed this situation with despair, but she eventually came to terms with it. "It is certain that they are going to amputate my right leg," she wrote in her diary. "I am very worried, but at the same time, I feel that it will be a liberation."[49] Following the surgery, Kahlo was fitted for an artificial leg, which she accepted with good humor.

To Kahlo's dismay, the amputation of her leg did not significantly reduce her pain or improve her health. She continued to depend on drugs to get through the day, and her behavior grew increasingly erratic. She eventually became depressed and considered suicide, as she admitted in her diary:

> They amputated my leg six months ago, they have given me centuries of torture, and at moments I almost lost my 'reason.' I keep on wanting to kill myself. Diego is the one who holds me back because of my vanity in

thinking that he would miss me. He has told me so and I believe him. But never in my life have I suffered more. I will wait a little while."[50]

Makes Her Exit

Kahlo made her last public appearance on July 2, 1954. Ignoring her doctors' orders, she attended a political demonstration in Mexico City. She and the other protesters were upset about U.S. intervention in the Central American nation of Guatemala. Although the people of Guatemala had chosen a Communist government in democratic elections, the United States had taken steps to remove that government from power because its policies were unfavorable to American business interests. As Rivera pushed Kahlo through the streets in a wheelchair, she appeared very pale and weak. A few days later, Kahlo celebrated her forty-seventh birthday with a small group of friends. All of this activity took a toll on her already fragile health, and she struggled with pneumonia and a high fever.

Kahlo died on the morning of July 13, 1954, in her bed at the Blue House in Coyoacán. The official death certificate listed the

Viva La Vida (Live Life Long) *was the last painting Kahlo completed before her death in 1954.*

At her funeral, Kahlo's coffin was draped with a Communist flag to show her loyalty to the Communist Party.

cause of death as a pulmonary embolism, or a burst blood vessel in her lung. But there were rumors that Kahlo had committed suicide by taking an overdose of pain medication. The final entry in her diary seems to suggest that she planned to kill herself, or at least that she expected to die soon. "I hope the exit is joyful—and I hope never to come back,"[51] she wrote.

On the other hand, the last painting that Kahlo completed before her death contains a clear message in celebration of life. *Viva La Vida (Long Live Life)* is a still life of bright red and green watermelons, some cut open and others whole. "It is crudely painted in a hand that is not too comfortable anymore with brush and paint, but its message of triumph is unmistakable—it is pure indomitable Frida,"[52] declared one critic.

Rivera had long realized that Kahlo's death was near. After all, she had given him a ring to mark their twenty-fifth wedding anniversary on the night before she died. They both knew that she would not live long enough to celebrate it on the actual date, two weeks later. Still, Rivera was not prepared for the intense emotions he felt during this time. "Too late now, I realized that the most wonderful part of my life had been my love for Frida,"[53] he recalled in his autobiography.

Kahlo Lives On

Friend, sister of the people, great daughter of Mexico: you are still alive…. You live on.

Andrés Iduarte, director of the National Institute of Fine Arts in Mexico City, speech at Kahlo's funeral titled "Imagen de Frida Kahlo," quoted in Hayden Herrera, *Frida Kahlo: The Paintings*. New York: HarperCollins, 1991, p. 223.

In the hours after Kahlo's death, her friends dressed her body in a colorful Tehuana costume and braided her hair. Mourners filed through the Blue House all day to pay their respects. That evening, her body was moved to the Palace of Fine Arts so that the public would have an opportunity to say farewell to the flamboyant artist.

During Kahlo's funeral, one of her loyal students, Arturo Garcia Bustos, draped a Communist flag over her coffin. Kahlo had been reinstated as a member of the Mexican Communist Party in 1947, and some of her last paintings included references to Communism and portraits of Russian leader Joseph Stalin. Although many witnesses felt that it was inappropriate to make a political statement at the funeral, Rivera refused to allow anyone to remove the flag. A short time later, the party reinstated Rivera as a member after an absence of twenty-five years.

More than five hundred mourners took part in Kahlo's funeral procession. At the end, her body was placed on an automated cart that carried it toward a large furnace to be cremated. In a bizarre scene that shocked many onlookers, the intense heat of the furnace caused Kahlo's body to rise up into a sitting position as it entered the flames. "In death as in life, Frida Kahlo forced her onlookers to confront the horror of the disintegration of the human body," noted one critic. "It was, as she probably would have seen it, her final work of art."[54] Afterward, Rivera took her ashes back to the Blue House, which he eventually turned into the Frida Kahlo Museum.

Chapter 6

Kahlo's Work Receives New Appreciation

During her lifetime, Frida Kahlo was known primarily as the flamboyant wife of Diego Rivera. She was often overshadowed by her famous husband, even though their paintings had completely different styles and themes. In the decades after her death, however, Kahlo's level of recognition and popularity increased significantly. In fact, her work attracted such a devoted worldwide following that she achieved legendary status in the world of art. Art historians even coined a new term, "Fridamania," to describe the remarkable surge of interest in Kahlo's life and work.

Her Work Highlights Strength

It isn't tragedy that governs Frida's work, as has been wrongly believed by many people. The darkness of her pain is merely a velvety background for the marvelous light of her biological strength, her superfine sensitivity, shining intelligence, and invincible strength to struggle for just being alive.

Diego Rivera, quoted in Raquel Tibol, *Frida Kahlo: An Open Life*. Translated by Elinor Randall. Albuquerque: University of New Mexico Press, 1993, p. 7.

Struggles for Recognition

When Kahlo died in 1954, at the age of 47, she had just started to be recognized as a major artist in her native Mexico. Throughout her career, she had faced an uphill battle to be taken seriously, for a number of reasons. Kahlo lived and worked during a time when there were not many women artists, for instance, so sexist attitudes caused some people to discount her paintings. She also worked in an era when murals were the most popular art form in Mexico, so her modestly sized paintings received less attention than they might have otherwise. Another factor in Kahlo's struggle for recognition was that her work was highly original and intensely personal, so many critics did not know what to make of it.

When Kahlo died in 1954 she was just beginning to come into her own as an artist.

First and foremost, though, Kahlo was often overshadowed by her husband, who was already one of Mexico's leading artists at the time they met and got married. Rivera's fame, along with the grand scale and public nature of his mural projects, distracted people's attention away from Kahlo's work for many years.

When Kahlo began showing her paintings in the 1930s, her connection to Rivera made it more difficult for her work to be taken seriously. Many critics seemed to think it was quaint that the famous muralist's wife wanted to be an artist. Some chose to focus on her flamboyant appearance or turbulent marriage instead of her work. Others insisted on comparing Kahlo's work to Rivera's or viewing the two artists as one unit.

When viewed objectively, however, their paintings were opposite in many ways. Rivera painted huge, wall-sized murals with a broad, historical focus. His work was often intended to serve a social or political purpose, by inspiring the poor people of Mexico to work toward building a better future. Kahlo, on the other hand, painted small, highly personal portraits that expressed her innermost feelings. The main purpose of her work involved exploring herself and giving meaning to her experiences.

The Frida Kahlo Museum

Despite their striking differences in style and content, Kahlo and Rivera were always loyally supportive of each other's work. They both thought that their spouse was Mexico's greatest artist and celebrated every success together. Rivera continued to promote Kahlo's work in the years following her death. He made plans to turn her longtime home, the Blue House in Coyoacán, into a museum honoring her life and art. He arranged for everything in the house to be preserved exactly as it had been on the day his wife died. Writing in his autobiography, Rivera also asked that "a corner be set aside for me, alone, for whenever I felt the need to return to the atmosphere which recreated Frida's presence."[55]

Rivera died of heart failure on November 24, 1957. His last will and testament contained a request that his body be cremated and his ashes mixed with Kahlo's and kept at the Blue House. His daughters did not honor his request, though. Instead, they accepted

A guest visiting Kahlo's studio. After her death, Rivera turned the Blue House into the Frida Kahlo Museum.

an invitation from the Mexican government to house his remains at the Rotunda of Illustrious Men in the Civil Cemetery of Sorrows.

Although it did not contain Rivera's ashes, the Frida Kahlo Museum opened to the public the following year. Since then, hundreds of thousands of people have visited the Blue House to see where Kahlo lived and worked. The museum features Kahlo's art studio and paints, the canopied bed where she spent so much time, her colorful Tehuana costumes and jewelry, her extensive collection of pre-Conquest art and retablo paintings, and her many books and letters.

Interest in Her Work Increases

While the opening of the Frida Kahlo Museum brought the artist to greater attention in Mexico, she remained relatively unknown in the larger world of art for two more decades.

Kahlo's embrace of Communism—and especially her support for the Russian dictator Joseph Stalin—made her unpopular in the United States during the 1950s. At this time, the United States and Soviet Union were involved in a period of intense political and military rivalry known as the Cold War, when each nation tried to expand its influence and spread its system of government around the world. Many Americans held strong anti-Communist feelings during this era.

The revival of interest in Kahlo's work began during the 1970s, when the women's liberation movement created more opportunities for women artists. Art historians started studying Kahlo's paintings around this time. Within the art community, Kahlo developed

Breaking New Ground as a Female Artist

In the early twentieth century, when Frida Kahlo decided to become a painter, there were few successful women artists to serve as her role models. Although many women possessed the desire and talent to make a career in art, they faced a number of obstacles to success. For instance, women were not allowed to attend art school in many countries, either due to simple discrimination or because various cultures deemed it inappropriate for women to see or draw nude human bodies.

As a result, women like Kahlo struggled to be taken seriously as artists and to gain recognition for their work. Before the women's liberation movement of the 1970s, noted the prominent art critic Lucy R. Lippard,

"The vast field of visual expression (with rare exceptions) had expressed only the visions, styles, and experience of one half of the population. There were plenty of women artists working, and working well. But most of them were making art in isolation. Their work was often limited to certain genres, submerged in false stereotypes, and blocked from representation by social and economic obstacles."

During her lifetime, Kahlo helped break through some of the barriers that prevented female artists from gaining recognition. Her strength and perseverance inspired later generations of women to build successful careers as artists.

Lucy R. Lippard, preface to *Contemporary Women Artists*. Detroit: St. James Press, 1999.

a reputation as a pioneer for being one of the first women artists to cover distinctly feminine themes in her work. For example, she painted pictures dealing with miscarriage, childbirth, and motherhood.

Kahlo came to greater popular recognition in 1983, when art historian Hayden Herrera published *Frida: A Biography of Frida Kahlo*. Readers in the United States and around the world were captivated by the story of Kahlo's physical suffering, turbulent marriage, passion for Mexico, and struggle for recognition as an artist. She gained many admirers for her ability to turn these challenges into compelling works of art. Herrera's book became a best-seller and launched Kahlo on a path to worldwide fame. As Herrera noted, "She became first a myth and then a cult figure."[56]

Work Appeals to Diverse Groups

As Kahlo became better known around the world, various groups of people found that they strongly identified with the artist and her paintings. Her work held widespread appeal among Hispanics, women, indigenous peoples, and people coping with pain, illness, or disability. "In a very short time in the context of the long history of art, her life and work have achieved an iconic status that actually competes with an artist like Michelangelo in its partisan intensity," explained one critic. "Different interest groups have gradually appropriated her for themselves."[57]

Over time, Kahlo has come to be considered one of Mexico's greatest artists. She expressed her passion for her country and its culture in everything she did, from her paintings to the way she dressed and decorated her home. One critic wrote:

> In her engagement with country and race, Frida is a very Mexican artist. In its habitual state of self-reflection—through a glass often very darkly—her painting mirrors many of the existential concerns and desires of her birthplace. Both artist and country are planted deep in the soil of their past, and like Mexico's, Frida's past was dramatic, bloody, and sad.[58]

For the Mexican people, as well as Hispanics in other parts of the world, Kahlo became a source of pride and a symbol of strength

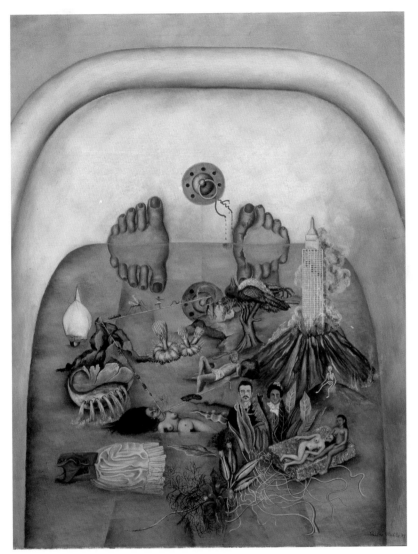

Because of paintings like What Water Has Given Me *(1939) Kahlo has come to be considered one of Mexico's greatest artists.*

and unity. "For many ordinary Mexicans Kahlo's suffering and art had come to symbolize Mexico's struggle against violence and the country's search for its own identity. Mexicans today still call Frida Kahlo 'the soul of Mexico.'"[59]

Kahlo has also served as a role model for women, and especially women artists. Feminists appreciate her bold and confrontational style, her rejection of traditional gender roles, and her openness about issues involving the female body and sexuality. "Kahlo made personal women's experiences serious subjects for art, but because of their intense emotional content, her paintings transcend gender boundaries," said Janet Landay of the Museum of Fine Arts in Houston. "Intimate and powerful, they demand that viewers—men and women—be moved by them."[60]

Some critics have questioned whether Kahlo is an appropriate choice as a feminist role model. They argue that, in many ways, Kahlo can be viewed as a victim of her circumstances rather than as a strong, independent woman struggling to overcome life's challenges. "In every possible sense, the mass-culture Kahlo embodies that now-poisonous term: victimhood," wrote one critic. "She was the victim of a patriarchal culture, victim of an unfaithful husband, and simply the victim of a horrific accident."[61]

Many other people, however, choose to celebrate the rebellious spirit that Kahlo showed throughout her life. "People always think of her as the tortured artist," said Julie Taymor, director of the 2002 film *Frida*. "I think what turns us all on is the humor and foul mouth and free sexuality of Frida—that's what makes her interesting."[62]

Fridamania

By the 1990s, Kahlo's widespread appeal had turned her into a legendary figure in the world of art. Her paintings sold for millions of dollars and appeared in the collections of many celebrities, including the pop singer Madonna. Kahlo's image appeared on the cover of *Time* magazine and on a U.S. postage stamp. Her popularity continued to increase with the publication of her diaries in 1995.

The phenomenon known as Fridamania continued into the 2000s. Record crowds turned out at museums worldwide to view exhibitions of her paintings. Many visitors attended the shows dressed in Tehuana costumes, with the space between their eyebrows penciled in to resemble Kahlo's famous unibrow. These avid fans purchased all sorts of memorabilia with Kahlo's image on it, including dolls, books, posters, T-shirts, jewelry, pins, mirrors, and mouse pads. "In the last 20 years, she's joined the rarefied ranks of artists like Picasso, whose work is as ubiquitous as wallpaper. More

In 2002, Kahlo's dramatic life story was made into a movie titled Frida *starring Salma Hayek.*

than just a poster girl for artsy adolescents or a Latina role model, Kahlo is now a coffee mug, a key chain, and a postage stamp."[63]

In 2002, Kahlo's dramatic life story became the subject of a major theatrical film, *Frida*. Directed by Julie Taymor, who also created the hit Broadway musical *The Lion King*, the movie stars Mexican actress Salma Hayek as Kahlo and Alfred Molina as Diego Rivera. The popular fascination with Kahlo continued in 2005, when PBS television aired a documentary called *The Life and Times of Frida Kahlo*. Directed by Amy Stechler, it provides insights into the artist's colorful and complex personality through personal photographs, home movie footage, and interviews with Kahlo's friends, students, and biographers.

Although some critics worry that Kahlo's remarkable appeal may have more to do with her tragic life story than her paintings, others dismiss this view. "The current view of Kahlo often fails to acknowledge that perhaps her images transcend autobiography and speak to universal themes, as all great art should,"[64] stated one reviewer. In addition, some experts believe that Fridamania has had a positive impact on young people's overall interest in and appreciation for art. "I don't necessarily think that the excessive popularity of an artist is a bad thing," said Gregorio Luke of the Museum of Latin American Art. "You can agree or disagree with the sideshow, the marketing of it all. But we need a younger generation to get involved in the art world, and she draws them in.... It's a fad, but a welcome one."[65]

Important Dates

1907
Magdalena Carmen Frieda Kahlo y Calderon is born on July 6 in Coyoacán, a suburb of Mexico City, Mexico.

1913
Kahlo contracts polio at age six and is confined to bed for several months. Although she recovers, her right leg is permanently disfigured.

1922
Kahlo is one of the first girls admitted to the National Preparatory School in Mexico City. She joins a rowdy group of students called the Cachuchas and plays tricks on artist Diego Rivera when he paints a mural at the school.

1925
Kahlo is seriously injured when the bus she is riding on the way home from school is hit by a trolley. The accident forces her to endure numerous surgeries and live in pain for the rest of her life.

1929
On August 21, Kahlo marries Diego Rivera.

1930
Kahlo accompanies her husband to the United States, where he completes mural projects in San Francisco, Detroit, and New York. Her feelings of homesickness and sadness over a miscarriage inspire her to develop her mature painting style during this time.

1934
Kahlo and Rivera return to Mexico. Their marriage suffers a major blow when Rivera has an affair with Kahlo's younger sister, Cristina.

1937

Kahlo and Rivera convince the Mexican government to allow exiled Russian Communist revolutionary Leon Trotsky to enter the country and serve as his hosts.

1938

Kahlo receives a solo exhibition at the Julien Levy Gallery in New York City.

1939

Kahlo travels to Paris for an exhibition of her paintings and is honored when the prestigious Louvre Museum purchases one for its permanent collection. After she returns home to Mexico, she and Rivera are divorced.

1940

Kahlo and Rivera remarry in San Francisco.

1943

Kahlo teaches art classes at the School of Painting and Sculpture in Mexico City.

1953

Kahlo is honored with her first solo exhibition in her home country.

1954

Kahlo dies on July 13, at the age of 47. The official cause of death is pulmonary embolism, but many people suspect suicide.

1958

The Frida Kahlo Museum opens at the Blue House in Coyoacán.

1983

Art historian Hayden Herrera publishes *Frida*, a major biography of Kahlo that becomes a best-seller and generates worldwide interest in the artist and her work.

Notes

Introduction: Expressing Feelings Through Art

1. Quoted in Bertram D. Wolfe, "Rise of Another Rivera," *Vogue*, November 1, 1938, p. 64.
2. Hayden Herrera, *Frida Kahlo: The Paintings*. New York: HarperCollins, 1991, p. 4.
3. Phyllis Tuchman, "Frida Kahlo," *Smithsonian*, November 2002, p. 51.

Chapter 1: Child of the Revolution

4. Quoted in Raquel Tibol, *Frida Kahlo: An Open Life*. Translated by Elinor Randall. Albuquerque: University of New Mexico Press, 1993, p. 39.
5. Quoted in Hayden Herrera, *Frida: A Biography of Frida Kahlo*. London: 1989, p. 20.
6. Andrea Kettenmann, *Frida Kahlo: Pain and Passion*. Koln: Taschen, 2003, p. 7.
7. Quoted in Tibol, *Frida Kahlo: An Open Life*, p. 37.
8. Hayden Herrera, *Frida Kahlo: The Paintings*, p. 7.

Chapter 2: A Life-Changing Accident

9. Quoted in Georgina Howell, "Frida Kahlo," *Harper's Bazaar*, November 2001, p. 234.
10. Quoted in Raquel Tibol, *Frida Kahlo: An Open Life*, p. 43.
11. Quoted in Phyllis Tuchman, "Frida Kahlo," *Smithsonian*, p. 51.
12. Quoted in Raquel Tibol, *Frida Kahlo: An Open Life*, p. 43.
13. Quoted in Raquel Tibol, *Frida Kahlo: An Open Life*, p. 51.
14. Antonio Rodriguez, "Frida Kahlo heroina del dolor," *in Hoy (Mexico City)*, February 9, 1952.
15. Andrea Kettenmann, *Frida Kahlo: Pain and Passion*, p. 19.
16. Georgina Howell, "Frida Kahlo," *Harper's Bazaar*, p. 234.
17. Melissa Chessher, *American Way*, December 1, 1990.
18. Quoted in Hedda Garza, *Hispanics of Achievement: Frida Kahlo*. New York: Chelsea House, 1994, p. 44.

19. *Diego Rivera, My Art, My Life*. New York: Citadel, 1960, p. 169.
20. *Diego Rivera, My Art, My Life*, p. 172.
21. Quoted in Gisele Freund, "Imagen de Frida Kahlo," *Novedades (Mexico City)*, June 10, 1951, p. 1.

Chapter 3: Artistic Style Matures in the United States

22. Phyllis Tuchman, "Frida Kahlo," *Smithsonian*, p. 51.
23. Hayden Herrera, *Frida Kahlo: The Paintings*, p. 48.
24. Quoted in Bambi, "Frida Es Una Mitad," *Excelsior (Mexico City)*, June 13, 1954, p. 6.
25. Quoted in Hayden Herrera, *Frida: A Biography of Frida Kahlo*, p. 131.
26. Quoted in Jill A. Laidlaw, *Artists in Their Time: Frida Kahlo*. New York: Franklin Watts, 2003, p. 21.
27. Quoted in Jill A. Laidlaw, *Artists in Their Time: Frida Kahlo*, p. 22.
28. Quoted in Hayden Herrera, *Frida: A Biography of Frida Kahlo*, p. 142.
29. Robin Richmond, Painters and Places: *Frida Kahlo in Mexico*. San Francisco: Pomegranate Artbooks, p. 96.

Chapter 4: Paintings Chronicle Her Turbulent Marriage

30. Quoted in Bertram Wolfe, *The Fabulous Life of Diego Rivera*. New York: Stein and Day, 1963, p. 357.
31. Hayden Herrera, *Frida Kahlo: The Paintings*, p. 112.
32. Quoted in Stephanie Mencimer, "The Trouble with Frida Kahlo," *Washington Monthly*, June 2002, p. 26.
33. Quoted in Phyllis Tuchman, "Frida Kahlo," *Smithsonian*, p. 51.
34. André Breton, "Frida Kahlo de Rivera" (exhibition catalog). New York: Julien Levy Gallery, 1938.
35. "Bomb Beribboned," *Time*, November 14, 1939, p. 29.
36. Quoted from an interview with El Universal, originally published on October 19, 1939, and included in Hayden Herrera, *Frida Kahlo: The Paintings,* p. 132.
37. Hayden Herrera, *Frida Kahlo: The Paintings*, p. 137.

38. Hayden Herrera, *Frida Kahlo: The Paintings*, p. 135.
39. Dr. Leo Eloesser, letter to Frida Kahlo, quoted in Hayden Herrera, *Frida Kahlo: The Paintings*, p. 153.
40. *Diego Rivera, My Art, My Life*, p. 242.
41. Hayden Herrera, *Frida Kahlo: The Paintings*, p. 155.
42. Robin Richmond, *Painters and Places: Frida Kahlo in Mexico*, p. 119.

Chapter 5: Art Reflects Kahlo's Declining Health

43. Quoted in Robin Richmond, *Painters and Places: Frida Kahlo in Mexico*, p. 20.
44. Hayden Herrera, *Frida Kahlo: The Paintings*, p. 180.
45. Quoted in Raquel Tibol, *Frida Kahlo: An Open Life*, p. 77.
46. Quoted in Stephanie Mencimer, "The Trouble with Frida Kahlo," *Washington Monthly*, p. 26.
47. Andrea Kettenmann, *Frida Kahlo: Pain and Passion*, p. 80.
48. Robin Richmond, *Painters and Places: Frida Kahlo in Mexico*, p. 137.
49. Quoted in Hayden Herrera, *Frida Kahlo: The Paintings*, p. 215.
50. Quoted in Hayden Herrera, *Frida Kahlo: The Paintings*, p. 218.
51. Quoted in Hayden Herrera, *Frida Kahlo: The Paintings*, p. 219.
52. Robin Richmond, *Painters and Places: Frida Kahlo in Mexico*, p. 139.
53. *Diego Rivera, My Art, My Life*, p. 285.
54. Georgina Howell, "Frida Kahlo," *Harper's Bazaar,* p. 234.

Chapter 6: Kahlo's Work Receives New Appreciation

55. *Diego Rivera, My Art, My Life*, p. 285.
56. Hayden Herrera, *Frida Kahlo: The Paintings*, p. 224.
57. Robin Richmond, *Painters and Places: Frida Kahlo in Mexico,* p. 10.
58. Robin Richmond, *Painters and Places: Frida Kahlo in Mexico,* p. 25.
59. Jill A. Laidlaw, *Artists in Their Time: Frida Kahlo*, p. 40.
60. Quoted in Phyllis Tuchman, "Frida Kahlo," *Smithsonian*, p. 51.

61. Stephanie Mencimer, "The Trouble with Frida Kahlo," *Washington Monthly*, p. 26.
62. Quoted in Joy Press, "Frida Icon: The Return of the Kahlo Cult," *Village Voice*, May 15-21, 2002.
63. Joy Press, "Frida Icon: The Return of the Kahlo Cult," *Village Voice*.
64. Stephanie Mencimer, "The Trouble with Frida Kahlo," *Washington Monthly*, p. 26.
65. Quoted in Stephanie Mencimer, "The Trouble with Frida Kahlo," *Washington Monthly*, p. 26.

For More Information

Books

Frida Kahlo, *The Diary of Frida Kahlo: An Intimate Self-Portrait*. New York: Abrams, 1995. Full of recollections, opinions, and sketches, the diary Kahlo kept during the last decade of her life provides a revealing look at the artist's feelings and motivations.

Hayden Herrera, *Frida: A Biography of Frida Kahlo*. New York: Harper and Row, 1983. Written by a prominent art historian, this is the definitive biography of Kahlo that helped bring the artist to worldwide acclaim.

Hedda Garza, *Hispanics of Achievement: Frida Kahlo*. New York: Chelsea House, 1994. A detailed biography of the artist, appropriate for junior high and high school students.

Jill A. Laidlaw, *Artists in Their Time: Frida Kahlo*. New York: Franklin Watts, 2003. A readable biography intended for elementary and junior high school students.

Periodicals

Georgina Howell, "Frida Kahlo," *Harper's Bazaar*, November 2001, p. 234. This article provides a brief overview of Kahlo's life and legacy.

Stephanie Mencimer, "The Trouble with Frida Kahlo," *Washington Monthly*, June 2002, p. 26. This article examines "Fridamania," the surge of interest in Kahlo's life and work that swept through the art world in the late 1990s and early 2000s.

Phyllis Tuchman, "Frida Kahlo," *Smithsonian*, November 2002, p. 51. Published to coincide with the release of *Frida*, a major theatrical film about Kahlo, this article places Kahlo's art in the context of her life and times.

Web Sites

Frida Kahlo and Contemporary Thought
(www.fridakahlo.it). A comprehensive source of biographical and critical information about Kahlo, with links to articles, galleries, and other resources.

Frida Kahlo—100 Years
(www.fridakahlofans.com). This extensive site offers a biography, photographs, timeline, list of works, bibliography, and quiz.

Mexico Connect, "The Frida Kahlo Museum"
(www.mexconnect.com/mex_/travel/grandall/grfridamuseo.html). This site provides a traveler's review of the Frida Kahlo Museum in Mexico City and an overview of information sources on the artist.

Films

The Life and Times of Frida Kahlo, PBS, 2005. Directed by Amy Stechler, this comprehensive documentary features personal photographs, home movie footage, and interviews with Kahlo's friends, students, and biographers.

Index

Picture Credits

Cover photo: Hutton Archive/Getty Images

AP Images, 23, 50, 58, 82, 87

Art Resource, NY. ©2007 Banco de México Diego Rivera & Frida Kahlo Museums Trust. Av. Cinco de Mayo No. 2, Col. Centro, Del. Cuauhtémoc 06059, México, D.F., 28

© Bettmann/Corbis, 22, 43, 77, 80

© Christie's Images/Corbis, 33, 48, 56

CNAC/MNAM/Dist. Réunion des Musées Nationaux/Art Resource, NY. ©2007 Banco de México Diego Rivera & Frida Kahlo Museums Trust. Av. Cinco de Mayo No. 2, Col. Centro, Del. Cuauhtémoc 06059, México, D.F., 61

Digital Image © The Museum of Modern Art/Licensed by SCALA/Art Resource, NY. ©2007 Banco de México Diego Rivera & Frida Kahlo Museums Trust. Av. Cinco de Mayo No. 2, Col. Centro, Del. Cuauhtémoc 06059, México, D.F., 65, 73

FPG/Hulton Archive/Getty Images, 36

Harlingue/Roger Viollet/Getty Images, 17

Hulton Archive/Getty Images, 10, 11, 15, 69

The Library of Congress, 21

Private Collection, Photo: Jorge Contreras Chacel/The Bridgeman Art Library International/©2007 Banco de México Diego Rivera & Frida Kahlo Museums Trust. Av. Cinco de Mayo No. 2, Col. Centro, Del. Cuauhtémoc 06059, México, D.F., 31

Private Collection/The Bridgeman Art Library International/©2007 Banco de México Diego Rivera & Frida Kahlo Museums Trust. Av. Cinco de Mayo No. 2, Col. Centro, Del. Cuauhtémoc 06059, México, D.F., 76

Schalkwijk/Art Resource, NY. ©2007 Banco de México Diego Rivera & Frida Kahlo Museums Trust. Av. Cinco de Mayo No. 2, Col. Centro, Del. Cuauhtémoc 06059, México, D.F., 39, 45, 63, 71, 85

About the Author

Laurie Collier Hillstrom is a partner in Northern Lights Writers Group, a free-lance writing and editorial services firm based in Brighton, Michigan. She has written and edited award-winning reference works on a wide range of subjects, including American history, biography, popular culture, and international environmental issues. Recent works include *Television in American Society Reference Library* (3 volumes, UXL/Gale Group, 2006), *War in the Persian Gulf Reference Library* (3 volumes, UXL/Gale Group, 2005), and *The Industrial Revolution in America* (9 volumes, ABC-Clio, 2005-07).